# BRITAIN'S
# LOST REGIMENTS

# BRITAIN'S
# LOST REGIMENTS

## THE ILLUSTRIOUS
## BANDS OF BROTHERS
## TIME HAS FORGOTTEN

### TREVOR ROYLE

Aurum
Press

First published in Great Britain
2014 by Aurum Press Ltd
74–77 White Lion Street
Islington
London N1 9PF
www.aurumpress.co.uk

A catalogue record for this book is available from the British Library.

ISBN 978 1 78131 188 2

1 3 5 7 9 10 8 6 4 2
2014 2016 2018 2017 2015

Typeset in Sabon by Saxon Graphics Ltd, Derby
Printed and bound by CPI Group (UK) Ltd, Croydon, CR0 4YY

# Contents

# Contents

# Introduction

The history of the British Army is really the story of its regiments and the men who served in them. From the very beginning they formed the backbone of a singular institution which is itself a reflection of the way the people of Britain view themselves and their collective past. The story began in 1660 when Charles II returned to London to retrieve the throne his father had been forced to vacate two decades earlier. At the time military institutions were not popular – people remembered only too well the years of Oliver Cromwell's Commonwealth and the rule of the major generals – but the new king had to be protected and the country had to be defended. Through a process of slow growth and frequent tardiness an army eventually came into being and from the outset it was based solidly on a regimental system which needed steady supplies of recruits to keep it in existence. Men joined up for many valid reasons such as a sense of duty, out of patriotism or a need for adventure, but not all motives were commendable. For every young man attracted by the chance to wear a uniform there would be many more who had broken the law or had fallen into debt or had fathered an illegitimate child. Another pressing impulse was that they had no option. In the poorest families an unemployed boy was an extra mouth to feed and in every regiment there were large numbers of young men who had been driven to escape grinding poverty by becoming soldiers. Others were simply coerced. The curious, the idle and the gullible were often pressed into service by smart recruiting sergeants who spun yarns of glory and honour and backed them up with ready supplies of alcohol. In that uncertain environment the regiment was all-important for inculcating a sense of continuity, structure and, above all, belonging.

Before too long, regiments were priding themselves on being as much a family affair as a military formation, providing their young recruits with the embodiment of home, perhaps the only home they would ever know. There was more to it, though, than a simple financial or social transaction. For all the rough and ready discipline, and for all the cheapness of the military life, there was a nobility to the soldier's calling. It might not have been popular among the wider public, and most civilians felt that the army was better kept out of sight and out of mind, but for those in uniform soldiering was an honourable profession that was open to all. From the late eighteenth century onwards infantry regiments were linked to their local communities and this was an important factor in encouraging recruitment and building up local pride. Regiments also reflected and played upon national and regional differences: solid English and Welsh county regiments consisting of tough and resilient men from the shires or the industrial towns, dashing Highlanders with their panoply of kilts and feathered bonnets and, everywhere, Irishmen serving a Crown they might not otherwise have supported. Not for nothing has it been said that the army and its regiments are the nation in uniform, for they are bound securely into the wider community, tied fast by bonds of affection, loyalty and pride that are difficult to break. 'Never forget,' said the eminent Field Marshal Archibald, Lord Wavell, 'the regiment is the foundation of everything.' Or, as Lord Moran, Winston Churchill's physician, put it equally succinctly in his great study, *The Anatomy of Courage*: all military training should lead soldiers 'to accept the religion of the Regiment – that only the Regiment matters'.

In return for that love of regiment soldiers have not always been well used by the politicians, perhaps because they were always only small in number and had little influence beyond the barracks and the battlefield. With the exception of the two world wars of the twentieth century the army rarely numbered more than 250,000 and by 2020 its numbers will have fallen to 82,000 regular soldiers, a poor reward, one would have thought, for all past endeavours. Over the years, periods of warfare have always been followed by times of peace when expenditure on the armed forces dropped, soldiers were made redundant and regiments, mainly infantry, were either disbanded or amalgamated, often with painful consequences for those affected. Even in recent times some regiments were raised specifically for wartime service to meet the needs of the hour – The Glider Pilot Regiment and The Reconnaissance Regiment of the Second World War come to mind – while others were lost almost absent-mindedly when penny-pinching became the order of the day. However, there is a case for saying that no regiment is ever entirely lost and that it will live on in men's minds as a mystical entity. The British Army certainly makes a great deal of the 'golden thread' which still links, say, the Middlesex 'Die-Hards' to the modern Princess of Wales's Royal Regiment, but the harsh reality is that those ties are only as strong as the men who made them. Like it or not, the old and bold soldiers are a dwindling band and once they have fallen out for the last time the regiments will be truly lost.

The key points in the story of the lost regiments are the following dates in which successive governments took momentous decisions to change the character and complexion of the army's infantry regiments:

1660: Restoration of the Stuarts and the disbandment of Cromwell's New Model Army followed by formation of the first standing army known as 'our guards and garrisons'.

1685: Monmouth's rebellion and the first expansion of the standing army. Infantry regiments named after their founding Colonels.

1751: Infantry regiments lose Colonel's names in their titles and are numbered in order of precedence under Royal Warrant.

1782: Infantry regiments without royal titles are provided with territorial titles to aid recruiting.

1858: European infantry regiments of the Honourable East India Company are placed under the authority of the Crown and are renumbered in the British Army three years later.

1873: Reform of the infantry system by Secretary of War Edward Cardwell and the introduction of a localisation scheme to aid recruiting by linking regiments in joint depots.

1881: Further reform of infantry system by Secretary of War Hugh Childers to form two-battalion regiments with territorial titles and with supporting Militia battalions.

1908: Formation of the Territorial Force (later Territorial Army).

1914: Expansion of the army to meet the manpower needs of the First World War. Line infantry regiments raise Service battalions for duration of hostilities and expand their Territorial battalions.

1922: Five Irish infantry regiments disbanded following the formation of the Irish Free State.

1947: Line infantry regiments lose their 2nd battalions.

1957: Announcement of the end of post-war National Service and reduction in size of army. Fifteen pairs of infantry regiments are chosen for amalgamation within fourteen brigades.

1968: Further reduction of the infantry to leave fifty battalions. New large regiments shed a battalion but there are still amalgamations and disbandments.

1990: Options for Change Defence review reduces size of army to leave thirty-eight battalions, including two of Gurkha Rifles, by losing seventeen of its fifty-five infantry battalions through further amalgamation.

2004: Future Infantry Structure review reorganises line infantry into twelve large regiments with varying numbers of Regular and Territorial battalions.

2010: Strategic Defence and Security review reduces the size of line infantry to thirty-two battalions. Four new large regiments lose a regular battalion through disbandment.

As can be seen, the main cull took place in the years after the Second World War when the army was steadily reduced in size as a result of financial belt-tightening and the introduction of improved weaponry. Between 1958 and 1961 its overall size came down to 185,000 and the infantry suffered most as the number of battalions was virtually halved. The need to supply personnel for the logistic and support services also meant that the infantry was less attractive as a career and young people reacted accordingly. To achieve those reductions regiments had to be amalgamated or disbanded and across the country the reforms sparked passionate and sentimental debate. In a rearguard action to prevent the introduction of a Corps of Infantry with numbered battalions, other expedients were tried – notably the raising of large regiments with battalions representing the old county regiments, and the creation of administrative brigades for smaller regiments – but soon these, too, had to be changed as the army steadily contracted. During this process a huge swathe was cut through the south and south-east of England with the result that local regiments such as The Buffs simply disappeared. By the beginning of the twenty-first century other parts of the country had followed, even in Scotland and the north of England where recruiting had remained reasonably buoyant. During this process illustrious names, previously resistant to change, such as The Black Watch, were removed unceremoniously from the army's Order of Battle.

A word needs to be said about the regiments that have been included in this volume. All were in existence in one form or another in 1881 at the conclusion of the far-reaching Cardwell/Childers reforms that gave the line infantry regiments their territorial structure – seventy-one infantry regiments with 141 battalions – and all survived into the second half of the twentieth century before facing disbandment or further amalgamation. (This accounts for the omission of The Green Howards, The Cheshire Regiment, The Royal Welch Fusiliers and The King's Own Scottish Borderers, all of which survived until 2006.) There is, though, an exception to this rule to take account of two infantry regiments whose histories are unique and which survived intact until the Future Infantry Structure review of 2004. The first is The Royal Scots, founded in 1633 and therefore the oldest line infantry regiment in the British Army. In 2006 it amalgamated with The King's Own Scottish Borderers (25th) to emerge as The Royal Scots Borderers, 1st Battalion The Royal Regiment of Scotland. The second is The Duke of Wellington's Regiment; the only line infantry regiment to bear the name of a commoner in its title, it also survived intact until the 2004 reforms when it became The 3rd Battalion, The Yorkshire Regiment. Otherwise the selection was made to represent the geographical spread of the United Kingdom and Ireland and to reflect the diversity of the many campaigns fought by the British Army over four centuries. Against that background the history of the British Army shows that the story of its regiments has been one of constant development, with cutbacks, amalgamations and changes of name being part of a process of evolution stretching back over several centuries. It would be fair to claim that in every case the development has not led to a diminution of the army's capabilities but has produced new regiments that are the equal of their predecessors.

For evidence of the character and fortitude of generations of soldiers who served in the army's line infantry regiments we need look no further than the countless Regimental Colours which are laid up in quiet places in county towns throughout Britain and Ireland. Hanging in cathedrals, churches or within the solemnity of regimental museums, they are all mute witnesses to the courage of men united in a common cause who did their duty uncomplainingly and unquestioningly, often accepting death and spurning dishonour, secure in the knowledge that their actions would live on in men's minds long after their passing. In just about every case those regiments have disappeared from the army's Order of Battle and their Colours are perhaps only idle curiosities to later generations, but in a brief verse attributed to the distinguished soldier-historian Lieutenant General Sir Edward Hamley it is possible to understand that some facets of military life are so potent that they can never perish:

> A moth-eaten rag on a worm-eaten pole,
> It does not look likely to stir a man's soul.
> 'Tis the deeds that were done 'neath the moth-
>      eaten rag,
> When the pole was a staff and the rag was a flag.

# The Royal Scots (The Royal Regiment)

## 1st

First of Foot, Right of the Line, The Royal Scots was the oldest line infantry regiment in the British Army, having been founded on 28 March 1633, and it enjoyed that distinction until 28 March 2006 when The Royal Regiment of Scotland came into being with five Regular battalions and two Territorial battalions. The new regiment's 1st Battalion was named The Royal Scots Borderers to perpetuate the titles of both The Royal Scots and The King's Own Scottish Borderers (25th), founded in 1689 as The Edinburgh Regiment, which drew its recruits from Scotland's Border counties. Given the great longevity of The Royal Scots it is not surprising that the regiment's best known nickname was 'Pontius Pilate's Bodyguard'. The origins are lost in the mists of time but the most credible version stems from a dispute involving the French Regiment of Picardy over the right of precedence – by longstanding military tradition the senior regiment always stands on the right of the line. While the two regiments were serving together in French service an officer in the Picardy Regiment employed the nickname 'Pontius Pilate's Bodyguard' as an insult and added for good measure that the Scots must have been asleep at their posts while guarding Christ's body after the crucifixion. 'You must be mistaken, sir,' retorted a Royal Scots officer, 'for had we really been the Guards of Pontius Pilate and done duty at the sepulchre, the Holy Body had never left it.'

As well as being the oldest infantry regiment in the British Army with a history of service to seventeen British monarchs – from King Charles I to Queen Elizabeth II – and a list of battle honours stretching back to the seventeenth century, the Royal Scots, or 'Royals', also have the distinction of serving two French kings, Louis XIII and Louis XIV. Following its formation in 1633 by Sir John Hepburn, an East Lothian landowner and mercenary soldier, the regiment was sent into French service as the Regiment de Hebron to fight in the Thirty Years War and did not return to Scotland until 1678 following the earlier restoration of Charles II. Throughout the eighteenth century the regiment saw almost continuous service fighting in Europe, North America and the West Indies. Its 2nd Battalion was part of the government army that defeated the Jacobites at the Battle of Culloden on 16 April 1746 and one of its private soldiers, Alexander Taylor, produced a graphic account of the fighting in a letter to his wife in which he described the 'most dreadful Havock' inflicted on the rebels.

During the campaigns against France in Europe the Royals played a prominent role and some engaging characters emerged from the ranks. Shortly before the Battle of Malplaquet, fought on 11 September 1709, one soldier named Donald McBain discovered that his wife had given birth to a son and then declared that she was leaving him. Nothing daunted, McBain put the three-week-old baby in his knapsack and both came through the fighting unscathed. (Not only did the Royals have the youngest participant in the battle, they also had the oldest in William Hiseland, a veteran of eighty-nine.) Master McBain (as Donald McBain was styled) also supplemented his income by running a fencing school and was frequently in trouble. In an incident in Edinburgh involving 'women and gaming', he outfought four assailants by giving one of them 'a Thrust in the Buttocks' and then escaping into the Fleshmarket. McBain later wrote an entertaining memoir of his life as a soldier.

Until the reforms of the British infantry between 1873 and 1881 the Royals had no specific base, but under the Cardwell/Childers reforms it became The Royal Scots (Lothian Regiment) with its main recruiting area designated as Edinburgh and the Lothian counties. A more enduring change was the establishment of a permanent depot at Glencorse in Penicuik to the south of Edinburgh, still an important military facility and now home to the 2nd Battalion The Royal Regiment of Scotland. Over the years much has changed at Glencorse but still standing are the memorial gates to the 11,213 Royal Scots who fell during the First World War. These were consecrated in 1927; five years earlier the Royal Scots Memorial Club had been opened in Abercromby Place in Edinburgh as a permanent and practical reminder of the regiment's sacrifices during the conflict. It is now a private establishment but still bears the regimental name.

During the First World War more than 100,000 men served in the regiment which fought on all the battlefronts except for Salonika and East and West Africa. A total of seventy-one battle honours were granted and six Royal Scots were awarded the Victoria Cross. Among them was

Bugler and privates of 2nd Battalion The Royal Scots in marching and drill order, Aldershot 1890. The Royals was the oldest line infantry regiment in the British Army.

Robert Dunsire, a miner from Fife, who showed exceptional courage and initiative during the Battle of Loos in September 1915 by twice going out into no-man's-land while under heavy enemy fire to bring in wounded comrades. He was later killed in a trench mortar attack and is buried in the Mazingarbe Commonwealth War Graves Cemetery near Lens in France.

One of the most compelling manifestations of the volunteer principle was the formation of the 15th and 16th Battalions, which were raised by two prominent Edinburgh businessmen, respectively Sir Robert Cranston and Sir George McCrae. Both battalions came into being in late 1914 and went on to serve on the Western Front but

In the 1970s and 1980s, at the height of the 'Troubles', 1st Battalion The Royal Scots was regularly deployed in Northern Ireland. A patrol of B Company receives orders on a street in Belfast.

McCrae's battalion was unique in that it contained a large number of footballers, most of whom played for one of the Edinburgh clubs, Heart of Midlothian, better known as Hearts. Shortly after the battalion was raised, one of the new recruits penned some verse for McCrae to read out when he appeared in uniform at a special performance of the annual Christmas pantomime at the King's Theatre, Edinburgh: 'Do not ask where Hearts are playing and then look at me askance. If it's football that you're wanting, you must come with us to France'. By then McCrae had recruited more than a thousand officers and men and his battalion assembled in Edinburgh's George Street on 15 December 1914, each volunteer being told to bring 'one pair good Boots, Topcoat, two pairs Socks, and shaving outfit'. The battalion saw action from the Battle of the Somme to the end of the war and suffered more than 800 casualties. In many respects, McCrae's was the original 'footballers' battalion': in addition to Heart of Midlothian, it also had players from Hibernian, Dunfermline Athletic and East Fife as well as from several junior clubs. (See also The Middlesex Regiment.) In 2004 a memorial cairn to McCrae's Battalion was unveiled in the village of Contalmaison on the Somme where it first went into action on 1 July 1916.

No less moving is the story of 7th Royal Scots, a Territorial battalion from Leith which was involved in a railway accident while on its way to serve in Gallipoli. The train carrying half the battalion collided with another train at Quintinshill Junction, near Gretna, in the early morning of 22 May 1915 and, as the survivors struggled to get clear, the wreckage was hit by an overnight express from London to Glasgow. Fires broke out and the death toll rose rapidly:

3 officers and 207 soldiers killed; 5 officers and 219 soldiers injured, and the battalion had to travel to Gallipoli at half strength. When the funerals were held in Leith's Rosebank Cemetery, Edinburgh's port area was in mourning with blinds drawn, shops closed and huge crowds lining the route of the funeral procession. At the time it was the biggest disaster in British railway history; it was, too, a terrible blow for a city which would soon be mourning even greater numbers of Royal Scots' casualties from Gallipoli and the autumn battles in Flanders.

The regiment's last major operational deployment came in 1991 when it was part of the UN forces sent to liberate Kuwait following the invasion ordered by President Saddam Hussein of Iraq.

---

## Battle Honours

### Pre-1914

*Carried on the Regimental Colour*
Tangier 1680, Namur 1695, Blenheim, Ramillies, Oudenarde, Malplaquet, Louisburg, Havannah, Egmost-op-Zee, St Lucia 1803, Corunna, Maheidpor, Busaco, Salamanca, Vittoria, St Sebastian, Nive, Peninsula, Niagara, Waterloo, Nagpore, Ava, Alma, Inkerman, Sevastopol, Taku Forts, Pekin 1860, South Africa 1899–1902

### First World War (35 battalions)

*Those in bold carried on the Queen's Colour*
Mons, **Le Cateau,** Retreat from Mons, **Marne 1914, 18,** Aisne 1914, Le Bassée 1914, Neuve Chapelle **Ypres 1915,**

**1917, 18,** Gravenstafel, St Julien, Frezenburg, Bellewaarde,
Aubers, Festubert 1915, **Loos, Somme 1916, 18,**
Albert 1916, 18, Bazentin, Flers-Courcelette, Le Transloy,
Ancre Heights, Ancre 1916, 18, **Arras 1917–18,** Scarpe 1917,
18, Arleux, Pilckem, Langemarck 1917, Menin Road,
Polygon Wood, Poelcappelle, Passchendaele, Cambrai 1917,
St Quentin, Rosieres, **Lys,** Estaires, Messines 1918,
Hazebrouck, Bailleul, Kemmel, Bethune, Soissonnais-Ourcq,
Tardenois, Amiens, Bapaume 1918, Drocourt-Queant,
Hindenburg Line, Canal du Nord, St Quentin Canal,
Beaurevoir, Courtrai, Selle, Sambre, France and Flanders
1914–18, **Struma,** Macedonia 1915–18, Helles, Landing at
Helles, Krithia, Suvla, Scimitar Hill, **Gallipoli 1915–16,**
Rumani, Egypt 1915–16, Gaza, El Mughar, Nebi Samwil,
Jaffa, **Palestine 1917–18,** Archangel 1918–19

## Second World War

*Those in bold carried on the Queen's Colour*
Dyle, **Defence of Escaut,** St Omer-La Bassee, **Odon,** Cheux,
Defence of Rauray, Caen, Esquay, Mont Pincon, **Aart,**
Nederrijn, Best, Scheldt, **Flushing,** Meijil, Venlo Pocket, Roer,
Rhineland, Reichswald, Cleve, Goch, **Rhine,** Uelzen, Bremen,
Artlenberg, **North-West Europe 1940, 44–45, Gothic Line,**
Marradi, Monte Gamberaldi, **Italy 1944–45,** South East Asia
1941, Donbaik, **Kohima,** Relief of Kohima, Aradura,
Schwebo, Mandalay, **Burma 1943–45**

## Post-1945 (1st Battalion)

*Carried on the Regimental Colour*
**Gulf 1991,** Wadi Al Batin

## Recipients of the Victoria Cross

Private Joseph Prosser, 2nd Battalion, Crimean War, 1855

Private Henry Howey Robson 2nd Battalion, First World War, 1914

Lance Corporal William Angus, 8th Battalion, First World War, 1915

Private Robert Dunsire, 13th Battalion, First World War, 1915

Captain Henry Reynolds, 12th Battalion, First World War, 1917

Private Hugh McIver, 2nd Battalion, First World War, 1918

Corporal (later Major) Roland Edward Elcock, 11th Battalion, First World War, 1918

Lieutenant David Stuart Macgregor, 6th Battalion, First World War, 1918

# The Queen's Royal Regiment (West Surrey)

## 2nd

For almost 300 years The Queen's Royal Regiment was the senior English line infantry regiment and second only to The Royal Scots in the order of precedence in the British Army. The regiment's other distinction is that it was raised in 1661 on Putney Heath (then in Surrey) by Henry Mordaunt, 2nd Earl of Peterborough, specifically to garrison the new English acquisition of Tangier in North Africa, which was part of Catherine of Braganza's dowry on her marriage to Charles II. For this service, it was also known as the Tangier Regiment in its early years and it is the only infantry regiment to have earned the battle honour 'Tangiers 1662–1680'. In 1684 it received its first royal title, becoming first The Queen's Regiment, then The Queen Dowager's Regiment (after Queen Catherine, Charles II's widow). A further change of title came in 1715 when it was renamed The Princess of Wales's Own Regiment of Foot after Princess Caroline of Ansbach, becoming The Queen's Own Royal Regiment of Foot twelve years later on the Princess of Wales's accession to the throne. Its final title, granted in 1921, was The Queen's Royal Regiment (West Surrey).

For most of its life a royal regiment, the Queen's also had a close connection with the county of Surrey which was its main recruiting area. In 1873 those links were formalised when Guildford was named as its depot with Stoughton Barracks opening three years later to house the regiment. Its imposing brick-built entrance and keep quickly became a local landmark and shortly thereafter the facility expanded dramatically with the further addition of married quarters and other accommodation. By the time the regiment received its new territorial title of The Queen's (Royal West Surrey Regiment) in 1881, Stoughton Barracks was home to 500 soldiers and their families. The depot became an important training centre and focus for recruitment in Surrey, and between 1945 and 1959 it was a primary training centre for National Service conscripts. Although Stoughton Barracks was finally closed in 1983 the buildings were sensitively renovated as luxury flats and named Cardwell's Keep. The links with the regiment were reinforced by the construction of a two-foot-high Paschal Lamb – the regimental badge – above the arch over the old road into the barracks. The regiment also has two memorial chapels in the town at Guildford Cathedral and Holy Trinity Church, which also contain memorials for those killed in action in the two world wars and the Boer War of 1899–1902.

As befits one of the oldest regiments in the British Army the Queen's have fought in most of the major conflicts, from the War of the League of Augsburg at the end of the seventeenth century to the Malayan Emergency in the 1950s. During that time six Victoria Crosses were awarded to soldiers serving in the regiment. Among the recipients was Captain (later Lieutenant General Sir) Bernard Freyberg, who was decorated while serving as

Recruits of The Queen's Royal Regiment (West Surrey) undergoing training at Stoughton Barracks in Guildford in May 1940. That same month the 'Phoney War' ended when the German Army invaded France and the Low Countries.

temporary commanding officer of the Hood Battalion of the Royal Naval Division at Beaucourt during the latter stages of the Battle of the Somme in November 1916. Born in Richmond, Surrey, Freyberg spent his childhood in New Zealand and it was fitting that he became its governor general between 1946 and 1952. He died in Windsor in 1963 and is buried in the churchyard of St Martha-on-the-Hill outside Guildford, Surrey. Perhaps the most extraordinary recipient was Lieutenant (later Brigadier) Wallace Duffield Wright who received the award while attached to the Northern Nigeria Regiment during the Kano-Sokoto Expedition, an operation mounted by Sir Frederick Lugard in 1903 to pacify the under-developed region of northern Nigeria. Commanding only forty-four men, Wright successfully fought off a force of around one thousand cavalry and infantry loyal to the Emir of Kano. Later Wright became a Member of Parliament and died at Chobham in Surrey in 1953 aged seventy-eight. His medal is on display at the regimental museum at Clandon Park, a National Trust property outside Guildford built between 1730 and 1733, for many years was the home of the Onslow family.

The most unusual task allotted to the regiment came in 1794 during the war against France when it was stationed at Dover guarding French prisoners of war. From that relatively easy duty the Queen's were ordered to join the warships HMS *Queen Charlotte*, HMS *Royal George*, HMS *Defence*, HMS *Majestic* and HMS *Russell* as Marines or 'sea soldiers' in the battle fleet commanded by Admiral Lord Howe. In this role they took part in the great naval victory off Brest known as 'The Glorious First of June' in which the French fleet was destroyed in little over two hours. On returning to Portsmouth, George III personally welcomed the victors home and ever after the Queen's enjoyed a close relationship with the Corps of Royal Marines, being accorded the Royal Navy's privilege of drinking the Loyal Toast while seated.

As was the case with every infantry regiment in the British Army the regiment expanded enormously during the First World War, drawing most of its recruits from Surrey. In addition to the Regular 1st, 2nd and 3rd battalions, there were nine Territorial Force battalions formed in Croydon, Guildford and Windsor, seven New Army or Service battalions raised in Guildford, Gravesend, Battersea, Lambeth and Brixton as well as six Labour or

Home Service battalions formed at Crawley, Balmer and Farnham. Following the outbreak of war in August 1914 there was no shortage of volunteers although one young man, John Kershaw, joined the Queen's on catching sight of its cap badge: 'Well to be quite honest about it, I asked to join a horse regiment, but they said they were all full up, and I looked up there where all the cap badges were and I thought this was a horse and I said yes that will do, and then of course I never saw a horse, it's a lamb!' Later he became a sergeant in the 1st Battalion and never regretted his decision, staying in the army for the rest of his working life and eventually becoming an In-Pensioner at the Royal Hospital, Chelsea. During the conflict the regiment lost over 8,000 casualties killed in action, mainly on the Western Front.

There was a similar reaction during the Second Word War. Although there were no Service battalions, the Queen's doubled the size of its Territorial battalions by the simple expedient of splitting each one in two and forming two brigades: 131 (Queen's) Brigade consisted of 1/5th, 1/6th and 1/7th Queen's and 169 (Queen's) Brigade was made up of 2/5th, 2/6th and 2/7th Queen's. The two brigades fought in France, North Africa and Italy while the Regular 1st and 2nd Battalions spent most of their war in Burma and saw some of the hardest fighting of the conflict. An extract from an unnamed officer's diary in the 1st Battalion gives a vivid impression of the dreadful conditions during the Battle of Kohima in May 1944: 'It is the most appalling mess I have ever seen. The red earth is torn and churned by thousands of shells pumped in to it during the four days, and the deeper craters, like filthy abscesses, are quickly being filled by muddy water.

Officers at luncheon in the field in 1900 during the Boer War when the 2nd Battalion formed 2nd Brigade, together with 2nd Devons, 2nd West Yorkshire and 2nd East Surrey. Photograph by Lieutenant L. D. Wedd DSO, 2nd Queen's Royal (West Surrey) Regiment.

Dead and smelling Japs are literally festooned on tree-stumps after the attacks of our Hurri-bombers [Hawker Hurricane fighter-bomber], and inside the flooded fox-holes lumps of flesh splash around.'

In 1959 the regiment amalgamated with The East Surrey Regiment (31st and 70th) to form The Queen's Royal Surrey Regiment. Seven years later this became the 1st Battalion, The Queen's Regiment, and in 1992 this large regiment amalgamated with The Royal Hampshire Regiment to form The Princess of Wales's Royal Regiment, which was named in honour of Diana, Princess of Wales. The end of The Queen's Royal Regiment was a case of death by a succession of cuts with the result that very little remains of the regiment other than soldiers' memories and a stubborn and understandable refusal to forget past glories.

---

## Battle Honours

### Pre-1914

*Carried on the Regimental Colour*
Tangier 1662–80, Namur 1695, Gibraltar 1704–05, Dettingen, Martinique 1794, Vimiera, Corunna, Talavera, Guadeloupe 1810, Albuhera, Salamanca, Vittoria, Pyrenees, Nivelle, Nive, Orthes, Toulouse Peninsula, Ghuznee 1839, Khelat, Afghanistan 1839, Cabool 1842, Moodkee, Ferozeshah, Aliwal, Sobraon, South Africa 1851–53, Sevastopol, Taku Forts, Pekin 1860, New Zealand, Afghanistan 1878–80, Suakin 1885, Burmah 1885–87, Tirah, Relief of Ladysmith, South Africa 1899–1902

## First World War (31 battalions)

*Those in bold carried on the Queen's Colour*
Mons, **Retreat from Mons**, Marne 1914, 18, Aisne 1914,
Ypres 1914, 17, 18, Langemarck 1914, Gheluvelt, Festubert
1915, Loos, **Somme 1916, 18**, Albert 1916, Bazentin, Delville
Wood, Pozieres, Guillemont, Flers-Courcelette, Morval,
Thiepval, Le Transloy, Ancre Heights, Ancre 1916, 18, Arras
1917, 18, Scarpe 1917, Bullecourt, **Messines 1917**, Pilckem,
Menin Road, Polygon Wood, Broodseinde, Passchenaele,
Cambrai 1917, 18, St Quentin, Bapaume 1918, Rosieres, Avre,
Billers Bretonneux, Lys, Hazebrouck, Bailleul, Kemmel,
Soissonais-Ourcq, Amiens, **Hindenburg Line**. Epehey,
St Quentin Canal, Courtrai, Selle, Sambre, France and
Flanders 1917, 18, Piave, **Vittorio Veneto**, Italy 1917, 18,
Suvla, Landing at Suvla, Scimitar Hill, **Gallipoli 1915**,
Rumani, Egypt 1915, **Palestine 1917–18**, Khan Baghdadi,
**Mesopotamia 1915–18, N.W. Frontier India 1916–17**

## Post-1918

*Carried on the Regimental Colour*
**Afghanistan 1919**

## Second World War

*Those in bold carried on the Queen's Colour*
Defence of Escaut, **Villers Bocage**, Mont Pincon, Lower Maas,
Roer, North-West Europe 1940, 44–45, Syria 1941, Sidi
Barrani, **Tobruk 1941**, Tobruk Sorte, Deil el Munasib,
**El Alamein**, Advance on Tripoli, **Medenine**, Tunis, North
Africa 1940–43, **Salerno**, Monte Stella, Scafati Bridge,
Volturno Crossing, **Monte Camino**, Garigliano Crossing,
Damiano, **Anzio**, Gothic Line, **Gemmano Ridge**, Senio Pocket,
Senio Floodbank, Casa Fabbri Ridge, Menate, Filo, Argenta

Gap, Italy 1943–45, **North Arakan, Kohima,** Yenangyaung 1945, Sittang 1945, Chindits 1944, Burma 1943–45

## Recipients of the Victoria Cross

Lieutenant (later Brigadier) Wallace Duffield Wright, The Queen's Royal West Surrey Regiment, attached Northern Nigeria Regiment, Kano-Sokoto Expedition, 1903

Captain (later Lieutenant General) Bernard Cyril Freyberg, The Hood Battalion, Royal Naval Division attached The Queen's Royal West Surrey regiment, First World War, 1916

2nd Lieutenant (acting Captain) Clement Robertson, The Queen's Royal West Surrey Regiment attached A Battalion Tank Corps, First World War, 1917

Lance Corporal John William Sayer, 8th Battalion, First World War, 1918

Captain (temporary Lieutenant Colonel) Christopher Bushell, 7th Battalion, First World War, 1918

Lieutenant Alec George Horwood, 1/6th Battalion attached 1st Northamptonshire Regiment, Second World War, 1944

# The Buffs (Royal East Kent Regiment)

## 3rd

Steady, The Buffs! This famous soldierly phrase is often thought to have been called out in the heat of battle to encourage the men of the Royal East Kent Regiment, better known as 'The Buffs'. It was certainly used by Rudyard Kipling in his novel *Soldiers Three* (1898) and has been uttered by a multitude of fictional characters, including Dorothy L. Sayers's gentleman detective Lord Peter Wimsey. But the origin is much more prosaic, if no less military.

It first came into use in 1858 while The Buffs were based in Malta where they shared the Florian Barracks with The 21st Royal North British (later Scots) Fusiliers. When the two regiments were on parade together the adjutant of The Buffs would call out: 'Steady, the Buffs, the Fusiliers are watching you!' This greatly amused the Scots who took to repeating the opening words of the order at every opportunity and the phrase soon passed into common usage not just in the army but among a wider public.

Formed originally from the Trained Bands of London, which were raised for service in the Netherlands during the reign of Elizabeth I, the regiment came into being in 1665 as the Holland Regiment of Foot but was soon nicknamed The Buffs on account of the buff leather facings on the soldiers' uniform jackets and the colour of their buff breeches. The official change in name came about in 1744 when the regiment was serving in the Netherlands during the War of the Austrian Succession and was under the command of Lieutenant General Thomas Howard. Fighting in the same campaign was the 19th Regiment of Foot, which was commanded by its Colonel, also called Howard – the Honourable Sir Charles Howard – and this might have caused confusion. At the time infantry regiments were named after their colonels and that would have made them both Howard's Regiment of Foot. As a result the two regiments took the Colours of their facings as part of their names – the 19th Foot became The Green Howards (a title it retained), while the 3rd Foot became Howard's Buffs, eventually being shortened to The Buffs.

In 1782 it received a territorial title, becoming the 3rd (East Kent) Regiment with two regular battalions, thereby cementing the lifelong connection with the county which became its main source of recruits. Throughout the regiment's existence its depot was situated in Canterbury, in the Victorian period a huge military garrison town with several infantry, artillery and cavalry barracks, all long since demolished.

The Garrison Church, now called All Saints, still stands in Military Road but the memorial chapel to The Buffs is in the south-west transept of Canterbury Cathedral, which is also known as the Warriors' Chapel. On the square lectern immediately inside the gate of the chapel are four books containing the names of 5,668 of all ranks of The Buffs killed in action in the First World War and

Sergeants of the 2nd Battalion The Buffs (East Kent Regiment)
pose near Bloemfontein during the Boer War, June 1900. Earlier
in the year the battalion had taken part in the successful Battle
of Paardeburg.

1,313 Buffs killed in action in the Second World War. Each day at 11 a.m., the ship's bell of the C-class light cruiser HMS *Canterbury* is rung and a page of one of the Books of Life is turned. The ceremony was initiated in 1926 when the smartest soldier on The Buffs Depot Quarter Guard marched from the barracks to the Cathedral and today the same duty is carried out by a former soldier of The Buffs.

Given its long history The Buffs has fought in most of Britain's wars but some actions were unique to the regiment. It served in the two government armies raised to put down the Jacobite uprisings in 1715 and 1745 and in that role was one of the fifteen regiments that fought in the government army at Culloden on 16 April 1746 when the Duke of Cumberland destroyed a Jacobite rebel force led by his cousin, Prince Charles Edward Stuart, also known as the Young Pretender.

Throughout its existence The Buffs commemorated 16 May as Albuhera Day to honour the role played by the regiment at the Battle of Albuhera during the Peninsular War in 1811. Although the result of the battle was indecisive, the regiment stoutly defended its Colours in two separate engagements. A heavy rainstorm having rendered the men's muskets useless at the start of the fighting, they were quickly surrounded by French cavalry who demanded their surrender. The fifteen-year-old officer carrying the Regimental Colour, Ensign Thomas, refused to obey, shouting out 'only with my life!' He was quickly cut down. Elsewhere on the battlefield Lieutenant Matthew Latham also refused to surrender the King's Colour despite being savagely struck with sabre blows. His body was later found on the battlefield with the Colour still safe inside his tunic; incredibly, he was still alive for all that he had been horribly wounded on his face and arms.

The other unique incident may be apocryphal but it, too, has passed into military legend. It concerns Private John Moyse, who served with the regiment in China during the Second Opium War (1856–60) and was taken prisoner following an attack on the Taku Forts in 1860. Ordered to kowtow (prostrate himself) before the Tartar Mandarin Tsan-koo-lin-sin, he refused and was swiftly executed. The incident prompted considerable excitement in the British press, especially in *The Times*, which hailed Moyse as an 'obstinate intemperate hero' who had refused to dishonour his country. Subsequently, doubts were raised about the authenticity of the incident, notably by the expedition's commander, General Sir Garnet Wolseley, but Moyse's reported courage gave rise to 'A Private of the Buffs', one of the great jingoistic poems of the Victorian age. Written by the poet Sir Francis Doyle, its triumphant conclusion summed up the patriotism which suffused the incident involving Moyse and the mandarin, real or imagined:

So, let his name through England ring –
A man of mean estate,
Who died, as firm as Sparta's King
Because his soul was great.

In 1881, as part of the army's reforms, the regiment strengthened its links with the county of Kent when a 3rd Militia battalion was formed from the East Kent Militia and composed of part-time volunteer soldiers from the local community. This change forced the regiment to lose its buff facings and to accept a new collar badge, the white

Brigadier General Charles van Straubenzee sitting (middle of photograph) with officers of the 3rd (East Kent) Regiment of Foot shortly after their arrival in the Crimea in May 1855. The regiment took part in the attack on the Quarries on 7 June and was also heavily involved in the second attack on the Redan on 8 September.

horse of Kent, but after loud protests these were withdrawn in 1894 and the buff facings and the traditional dragon badge were restored. Following distinguished service in the First World War, when the regiment raised fifteen battalions, The Buffs were awarded the royal title as part of the honours conferred by George V on his Silver Jubilee in 1935. However, the regiment already had a regal connection, albeit with the Royal House of Denmark. In the early days its Colonel-in-Chief was Prince George of Denmark (1689–1708), the consort of Queen Anne. This tradition was continued in the twentieth century with the appointment of three members of the Danish Royal Family to the same position, namely Frederick VIII of Denmark (1906–14), Christian X of Denmark (1914–47) and Frederick IX of Denmark (1947–61).

But all that history and all those royal connections could not save The Buffs. The long drawn-out process of closure began in 1961 when they amalgamated with The Queen's Own Royal West Kent Regiment (50th and 97th) to form The Queen's Own Buffs, The Royal Kent Regiment. There were more cuts to come: five years later, on the last day of 1966, without any ceremony, The Queen's Regiment was formed, with The Queen's Own Buffs becoming its 2nd Battalion. As if that were not sufficient indignity for a regiment that could look back on three centuries of history, the process continued in 1992 when The Queen's Regiment amalgamated with The Royal Hampshire Regiment to form The Princess of Wales's Royal Regiment. A link with the past was maintained by situating the regimental headquarters in Canterbury but by then the cry 'Steady The Buffs' was an echo from the irretrievable past.

# Battle Honours

## Pre-1914

*Carried on the Regimental Colour*
**Blenheim, Ramilles, Oudenarde, Malplaquet, Dettingen, Guadeloupe, 1759, Belleisle, Douro, Talavera, Albuhera, Vittoria, Pyrenees, Nivell, Nive, Orthes, Toulouse, Peninsula, Punniar, Sevastopol, Taku Forts, South Africa 1879, Chitral, Relief of Kimberely, Paardeberg, South Africa 1900–02**

## First World War (15 battalions)

*Those in bold carried on the Queen's Colour*
Aisne 1914, **Armentieres 1914, Ypres 1915, 17,** Gravenstafel, St Julien, Frezenberg, Bellewaarde, Hooge 1915, **Loos, Somme 1916, 18,** Bazentine, Delville Wood, Pozieres, Flers-Courcelette, Morval, Thiepval, Le Transloy, Ancre Heights, Ancre 1916, 18, **Arras 1917,** Scarpe 1917, Messines 1917, Pilckem, Passchendaele, Cambrai 1917, 18, St Quentin, Ayre, **Amiens,** Bapaume 1918, **Hindenburg Line,** Epehy, St Quentin Canal, Selle, Sambre, France and Flanders 1914–18, **Struma,** Douran 1918, Macedonia 1915–18, Gaza, **Jerusalem,** Tell Asur, Palestine 1917–18, Aden, Tigris 1916, Kut al Amara 1917, **Baghdad,** Mesopotamia 1915–18

## Second World War

*Those in bold carried on the Queen's Colour*
Defence of Escaut, St Omer-La Bassee, Withdrawal to Seine, **North-West Europe 1940,** Sidi Suleiman, **Alem Hamza,** Alam el Halfa, **El Alamein,** El Agheila, Advance on Tripoli, Tebaga Gap, El Hamma, Akarit, Djebal Azzag 1943, **Robaa Valley,** Djebel Bech, Heidows, Medjez Plain, Longstop Hill 1943, North Africa 1941–43, Centuripe, Monte Rivoglia, **Sicily 1943,** Termoli, **Trigno,** Sangro, **Anzio,** Cassino I, Liri Valley,

Aquino, Rome, Trasimene Line, Coriano, Monte Spaduro, Senio, **Argenta Gap**, Italy 1943–45, **Leros**, Middle East 1943, Malta 1940–42, **Shwell**, Myitson, Burma 1945

## Recipients of the Victoria Cross

Major (Brevet Lieutenant Colonel, later General) Frederick Francis Maude, 3rd Regiment, Crimean War, 1855

Private (later Corporal) John Connors, 3rd Regiment, Crimean War, 1855

Corporal (later Colour Sergeant) James Smith, The East Kent Regiment, First Mohmand Campaign, 1897

Lance Corporal (acting Corporal) William Reginald Cotter, 6th Battalion, First World War, 1916

# The Royal Northumberland Fusiliers

## 5th

Renowned as the 'Fighting Fifth', The Royal Northumberland Fusiliers had a proud history of active service,
with a list of sixty-seven battle honours running from
Wilhelmsthal in 1762 during the Seven Years War (a
battle honour unique to the regiment) to Imjin during the
Korean War of 1950–53. With its distinctive red over
white hackle and grenade cap badge, the regiment was
always instantly recognisable but, as successive
generations of soldiers have argued, deeds rather than
details of uniform matter. The regiment was raised in
1674 for service with the army of the Dutch Republic and
was known as the Irish Regiment, or Clare's Regiment,
after its founder, Daniel O'Brian, 3rd Viscount Clare,
who was attainted in 1691 after supporting the claims of
James II against William of Orange. He was succeeded as
Colonel by Sir John Fenwick, of Wallington in
Northumberland, but he did not last long either, being
attainted and then executed for his support of the Jacobite
cause. In 1685 the regiment joined the English military
establishment, adopting St George and the dragon as its
emblem and using it on its Regimental Colour and drums
instead of the more usual Royal Cypher employed by
other line infantry regiments.

It was not until 1782, by which time it had become the 5th Regiment of Foot, that the regiment cemented its association with the county of Northumberland as a compliment to its Colonel, Hugh Percy, 1st Duke of Northumberland, a prominent Northumbrian landowner. A further change came on 4 May 1836 when William IV ordered that the regiment should be designated as Fusiliers, a singular honour that had its origins in the development of the infantry regiments of the British Army – originally Fusiliers were armed with the flintlock fusil instead of the more common matchlock musket and were specialist infantrymen who guarded the artillery train.

By then the regiment's links with Northumberland were well established. Not only did it use part of Alnwick Castle as its depot but during the American War of Independence its Colonel was Hugh, Earl Percy, soon to become 2nd Duke of Northumberland. Although unprepossessing in appearance – he suffered from gout and had poor eyesight – young Percy was a professional soldier to his fingertips and entertained radical ideas about the military profession. In particular his views on discipline were ahead of their time, prompting one observer to note: 'He detested corporal punishments. At a time when other commanders were resorting to floggings and firing squads on Boston Common, he led his regiment by precept and example.'

Perhaps the most unusual soldier during the regiment's deployment in North America was Phoebe Hessel, from Stepney in London, who disguised herself as a man in order to be with her lover, Samuel Golding, a soldier in the 5th Foot. She fought at the Battle of Fontenoy in 1745, where she was wounded in the arm, but her prior identity was discovered when she was stripped to the waist prior to being flogged as part of a punishment. Although she said 'strike and be damned' she was instead admonished and duly discharged. In her retirement she married Golding and they had nine children. She then moved to Brighton where she became a local celebrity and received a pension from the Prince Regent. Phoebe Hessel died in 1821 at the grand old age of 108.

On returning from America, the regiment played a prominent role in the Peninsular War, during which it gained a new nickname, 'Lord Wellington's Bodyguard', bestowed upon it because of great courage displayed while beating off a determined French attack at El Bodón in 1811. In his despatches Wellington described the regiment's action as a 'memorable example of what can be done by steadiness, discipline, and confidence'. Later in the century, in 1857, the regiment served during the Indian Mutiny, receiving the battle honour 'Lucknow', and it also fought in the Second Afghan War of 1878–80. In the former campaign in India the regiment received the first of nine Victoria Crosses won by men of The Northumberland Fusiliers. These were awarded to Patrick McHale and Peter McManus during the relief of the garrison at Lucknow. As with so many soldiers in English and Scottish regiments at that time, both men were Irish: McHale was from Killala in County Mayo, McManus from Tynan in County Armagh. Both medals were awarded for courage under fire but each occurred in different circumstances: on 26 September McManus provided covering fire for a party of wounded men after the building in which they were sheltering was set on fire; during the capture of the Cawnpore Battery, McHale

Men of 1st Battalion The Northumberland Fusiliers after the Battle of St Eloi on 27 March 1916. Following the detonation of several mines under the German lines, the attacking troops rushed to take the craters. Although the initial advance went well, the attack eventually became bogged down in the waterlogged landscape.

seized a rebel gun at Alum Bagh and turned it on the retreating mutineers. However, service in India came at a price: during the twenty years that the regiment served on the subcontinent 232 of their number succumbed to disease, many of them without hearing a shot fired in anger.

When the First World War broke out in 1914, the Fighting Fifth expanded enormously, raising fifty-two battalions, twenty-nine of which served overseas. Making full use of the numbers of Scots and Irish who worked in the north-east, the regiment raised four battalions (20th to 23rd Northumberland Fusiliers), which served as the Tyneside Scottish Brigade, and a further four (24th to 27th Northumberland Fusiliers), which served as the Tyneside Irish Brigade. A member of the organising committee noted that when the Tyneside Scottish battalions were recruited 'there could be no more moving spectacle than that afforded by bodies of men marching into Newcastle from outlying villages for enlistment in the Brigade; one group of about ninety miners so marching nine or ten miles into the city headed by some of their men playing mouth organs'.

Both brigades saw action at the Battle of the Somme where they sustained heavy casualties. After the war the Colours of the Tyneside Irish were laid up in Newcastle's Cathedral Church of St Mary. One of its men, Lance Corporal Thomas Bryan, had played rugby league for Castleford before the war and was awarded the Victoria Cross after he knocked out a German machine-gun position during the Battle of Arras in April 1917. The enthusiasm of the men of the north-east to join up came at a heavy price: during the First World War, The

Northumberland Fusiliers suffered some 16,000 casualties, one of the highest regimental totals in the British Army. Their sacrifice is commemorated by the City War Memorial in Old Eldon Square in Newcastle and also by 'The Response' memorial which shows soldiers marching off to war beneath the figure of a winged angel. It stands in the grounds of the Church of St Thomas the Martyr and was erected from funds provided by the shipping magnate Sir George Renwick whose sons served in The Northumberland Fusiliers. In 1935 the regiment received a royal title, becoming The Royal Northumberland Fusiliers.

The regiment's proud history came to an end in 1968 when it became the 1st Battalion of The Royal Regiment of Fusiliers but, fittingly, it was in action to the very last. In 1950 it formed part of 29 Infantry Brigade in the Korean War along with 1st Gloucestershire Regiment and 1st Royal Ulster Rifles; and in 1967 it was one of the last regiments to leave the British colony of Aden. Towards the end of its tour in June, 1st Royal Northumberland Fusiliers lost four men when a joint patrol was ambushed by mutinous members of the Aden police force.

Unlike most other infantry regiments The Royal Northumberland Fusiliers possessed a third colour in honour of its conduct at the Battle of Wilhelmsthal which was carried on parade by a drummer every St George's Day. On amalgamation, the Regimental Colours were laid up in the Cathedral Church of St Nicholas in Newcastle. The regimental museum is located in Abbot's Tower at Alnwick Castle.

Full dress parade of 1st Battalion The Northumberland Fusiliers in Portsmouth in January 1914. Eight months later the battalion had crossed over to France as part of the British Expeditionary Force and was in action in the opening Battle of Mons.

# Battle Honours

## Pre-1914

*Carried on Regimental Colour*
**Wilhelmsthal, St Lucia, 1778, Rolica, Vimiera, Corunna, Busaco, Salamanca, Badajoz, Ciudad Rodrigo, Vittoria, Nivelle, Orthes, Toulouse, Peninsula, Lucknow, Afghanistan 1878–80, Khartoum, Modder River, South Africa 1899–1902**

## First World War (52 battalions)

*Those in bold carried on Queen's Colour*
**Mons**, Le Cateau, Retreat from Mons, **Marne 1914**, Aisne 1914,18, La Bassée 1914, Messines 1914, 17, 18, Armentières 1914, **Ypres 1914, 15, 17, 18**, Nonne Bosschen, Gravenstafel, **St. Julien**, Frezenberg, Bellewaarde, Loos, **Somme 1916, 18**, Albert 1916, 18, Bazentin, Delville Wood, Pozières, Flers-Courcelette, Morval, Thiepval, Le Transloy, Ancre Heights, Ancre 1916, Arras 1917, 18, **Scarpe 1917, 18**, Arleux, Pilckem, Langemarck 1917, Menin Road, Polygon Wood, Broodseinde, Passchendaele, Cambrai 1917–18, St. Quentin, Bapaume 1918, Rosières, Lys, Estaires, Hazebrouck, Bailleul, Kemmel, Béthune, Scherpenberg, Drocourt Quéant, Hindenburg Line, Épéhy, Canal du Nord, St. Quentin Canal, Beaurevoir, Courtrai, **Selle**, Valenciennes, Sambre, France and Flanders 1914–18, **Piave**, Vittorio Veneto, Italy 1917–18, **Struma**, Macedonia 1915–18, **Suvla**, Landing at Suvla, Scimitar Hill, Gallipoli 1915, Egypt 1916–17

## Second World War

*Those in bold carried on Queen's Colour*
Defence of Escaut, Arras Counter Attack, St. Omer-La Bassée, **Dunkirk 1940**, Odon, **Caen**, Cagny, Falaise, Nederrijn,

**Rhineland,** North-West Europe 1940, 44–45, **Sidi Barrani, Defence of Tobruk, Tobruk 1941,** Belhamed, **Cauldron,** Ruweisat Ridge, **El Alamein,** Advance on Tripoli, Medenine, North Africa 1940–43, **Salerno,** Volturno Crossing, Monte Camino, Garigliano Crossing, **Cassino II,** Italy 1943–45, Singapore Island

## Post-1945 (1st Battalion)

*Carried on Regimental Colour*
Seoul, **Imjin,** Kowang-San, **Korea 1950–51**

## Recipients of the Victoria Cross

Private Robert Grant, 5th Regiment Indian Mutiny, 1857
Private Patrick McHale, 5th Regiment, Indian Mutiny, 1857
Sergeant Peter McManus, 5th Regiment, Indian Mutiny, 1857
Private Ernest Sykes, 27th Battalion, First World War, 1917
Lance Corporal Thomas Bryan, 25th Battalion, First World War, 1917
2nd Lieutenant James Bulmer Johnson, 36th Battalion, First World War, 1918
Private Wilfred Wood, 10th Battalion, First World War, 1918
2nd Lieutenant John Scott Youll, 1st Battalion, First World War, 1918
Captain James Joseph Bernard Jackman, 1st Battalion, Second World War, 1941

# The Royal Fusiliers
## (City of London Regiment)

## 7th

London, the nation's capital, is synonymous with Britain's military traditions. It is home to the Horse Guards, once the headquarters of the British Army, and nearby Wellington Barracks houses the headquarters of the five regiments of Foot Guards – Grenadier, Coldstream, Scots, Irish and Welsh. The city also has its own infantry regiment, The Royal Fusiliers, which was founded by James II on 11 June 1685 as Our Royal Regiment of Fuzileers under the command of George Legge, later Lord Dartmouth, Master General of the Ordnance. Four decades earlier, the regiment's origins can be traced back to the Trained Bands of the Tower of London and its Hamlets, which had been raised in 1648 at the command of Oliver Cromwell to form the Tower Guard and to guard the Ordnance Train as part of the New Model Army. That specialist role was continued in the new regiment which was also known for a short time as Our Ordnance Regiment: each man was armed with a 'fusil', a recently developed French design of musket with a covered flash-pan which made it safer to use near ammunition carts containing open barrels of gunpowder. The Fusiliers were the first English regiment of foot to be granted the title 'Royal' and its badge was adopted from the traditional royal emblem marked upon all the king's or queen's ordnance of war – the united red and white rose within the Garter and surmounted by the Crown. The Tower of London was its original headquarters and the historic building was always associated with the regiment – it houses the modern regimental museum – although the depot was moved to Hounslow in west London at the time of the Cardwell/Childers reforms in the 1870s.

As was the case with all line infantry regiments of the period, the Royal Fusiliers spent much of its time fighting abroad, firstly in France and Flanders and then in North America during the American War of Independence where the regiment was all but wiped out in the disastrous Battle of Cowpens in 1781 – the first time British Regular forces were beaten in a set battle by American Irregular soldiers. Better fortune followed in the war against Napoleon where the regiment gained ten battle honours during the Peninsular War and, by the time of the Crimean War, Sergeant Timothy Gowing was able to record with pride that he had joined 'one of the smartest regiments of our army ... I selected this regiment for its noble deeds of valour under Lord Wellington in the Peninsula.' Gowing's memoirs are among the most vividly realised of the Victorian period and the type of man he admired in the Fusiliers must have included Lieutenant William Hope, who was awarded the Victoria Cross for his courage in bringing in wounded men during the attack on the Redan at Sevastopol, all the while under heavy enemy fire. The son of the Lord Chief Justice Clerk of Scotland, Hope was a natural soldier who reached the rank of Colonel, but he retired from the army and became an enthusiastic

Men of 1st Battalion The Royal Fusiliers march through Wiesbaden in December 1929 during their service with the British Army of the Rhine, which had been created ten years earlier to implement the British occupation of the Rhineland.

supporter of the Volunteer movement, becoming in time the commanding officer of the 1st City of London Artillery Volunteers. He was also the inventor of the shrapnel shell for rifled guns.

Throughout its existence the City of London was important to the life of The Royal Fusiliers and to its successor, The Royal Regiment of Fusiliers. It enjoys close links with the Lord Mayor, providing a detachment for the procession to mark his installation, and by tradition Fusilier officers have entertained the Lord Mayor at the 'City Luncheon' towards the end of his mayoralty by way of thanks for the City's support for its regiment. The regimental chapel in London is the Chapel Royal of St Peter ad Vincula within the Tower of London and it is here that the Regimental Colours hang. Other sites devoted to the regiment include the regimental Memorial Chapel situated in the Church of the Holy Sepulchre at Holborn Viaduct, London, and the Garden of Remembrance on the north side of the church. Also in Holborn is the striking memorial to the 21,941 fusiliers who died in action during the First World War; this takes the form of a pedestal of Portland stone below a bronze figure of a Royal Fusilier standing with rifle as if defending the entrance to the city. Executed by the sculptor Albert Toft, the model for the fusilier was Sergeant Cox, who had served in the regiment throughout the war.

During the conflict the Royal Fusiliers raised forty-seven battalions for service in addition to four Fusilier-badged battalions of the Territorial Force which served with the London Regiment. Many of the battalions were specially raised for war service and had business, sporting or educational affiliations, such as the 18th, 19th, 20th and 21st battalions which formed the University and Public Schools Brigade at Epsom at the beginning of the war. Within eleven days, 5,000 young university and public school men had joined its ranks and onlookers remarked on their 'soldierly appearance, splendid marching and soldierly physique'. Among their number was Hopkin Maddock, an Old Boy of Christ College Brecon who played rugby for London Welsh and had won six international caps for Wales. The brigade crossed over to France in November 1915 and immediately suffered heavy casualties, the 20th Battalion being virtually wiped out during the fighting at High Wood during the Battle of the Somme. It was a noble and patriotic undertaking but old regular soldiers such as Frank Richards were not always impressed. 'They were very decent chaps, but hopeless as soldiers,' he noted in his autobiography. 'The only thing they ever became proficient in was swearing.' Other specialist battalions were the 10th Stockbrokers' Battalion and the 23rd and 24th Sportsmen's Battalions, but the most singular of the war-raised battalions must have been those numbered 38th to 42nd which later served as the Jewish Legion in Palestine.

Both the 1st and 2nd Battalions saw service in the Second World War, fighting in North-West Europe, the Middle East and Italy. Perhaps the most unusual Fusilier of this war was Johnny Ramensky, a Scot of Lithuanian extraction and an infamous burglar and safe-breaker known for never resorting to violence in his 'trade'. In 1943 while doing time in Peterhead Prison, 'Gentleman Johnny' was given an option: stay in prison or join the army. He chose the latter. After serving in the Royal Fusiliers he joined the Commandoes as an instructor and conducted a number of daring raids, behind enemy lines, including one on the headquarters of General Rommel in North Africa to capture sensitive documents.

In the post-war period the regiment served in Korea as part of the US-led operations against North Korean and Chinese forces. Among those who saw action in the front line was Maurice Micklewhite (who would become better known as the actor Michael Caine), born in Bermondsey but brought up in Southwark, south London. Far from leaving him disillusioned, the experience made him a lifelong supporter of conscription as a means of combating youth crime in Britain: 'I'm just saying, put them in the army for six months. You're there to learn how to defend your country. You belong to the country. Then when you come out, you have a sense of belonging rather than a sense of violence.' Other Fusiliers who went on to enjoy successful careers in show business included band leader Billy Cotton, who also flew as a pilot in the Royal Flying Corps, and the actor Leslie Grantham, who played the character 'Dirty Den' in the television soap opera *EastEnders*.

On St George's Day 1968 the regiment became part of The Royal Regiment of Fusiliers following the amalgamation of The Royal Northumberland Fusiliers, The Royal Warwickshire Fusiliers, The Royal Fusiliers and The Lancashire Fusiliers. A link with the past was maintained when the Tower of London became the new regiment's London area headquarters.

Men of 9th Battalion The Royal Fusiliers at an observation post
at the window of a ruined house during the fighting in Sicily,
12 September 1943.

## Battle Honours

### Pre-1914

*Carried on the Regimental Colour*

**Namur 1695, Martinique 1809, Talavera, Busaco, Albuhera, Badajoz, Salamanca, Vittoria, Pyrenees, Orthes, Toulouse, Peninsula, Alma, Inkerman, Sevastopol, Kandahar 1880, Afghanistan 1879–80, Relief of Ladysmith, South Africa 1899–1902**

### First World War (47 battalions)

*Those in bold carried on the Queen's Colour*

**Mons**, Le Cateau, Retreat from Mons, **Marne 1914**, Aisne 1914, La Bassée 1914, Messines 1914, 17, Armentières 1914, **Ypres 1914, 15, 17, 18**, Nonne Bosschen, Gravenstafel, St. Julien, Frezenberg, Bellewaarde, Hooge 1915, Loos, **Somme 1916, 18**, Albert 1916, 18, Bazentin, Delville Wood, Pozières, Flers-Courcelette, Thiepval, Le Transloy, Ancre Heights, Ancre 1916, 18, **Arras 1917, 18**, Vimy 1917, Scarpe 1917, Arleux, Pilckem, Langemarck 1917, Menin Road, Polygon Wood, Broodseinde, Poelcappelle, Passchendaele, **Cambrai 1917, 18**, St. Quentin, Bapaume 1918, Rosières, Avre, Villers Bretonneux, Lys, Estaires, Hazebrouck, Béthune, Amiens, Drocourt-Quéant, **Hindenburg Line**, Havrincourt, Épéhy, Canal du Nord, St. Quentin Canal, Beaurevoir, Courtrai, Selle, Sambre, France and Flanders 1914–18, Italy 1917–18, **Struma**, Macedonia 1915–18, Helles, **Landing at Helles**, Krithia, Suvla, Scimitar Hill, Gallipoli 1915–16, Egypt 1916, Megiddo, Nablus, **Palestine 1918**, Troitsa, Archangel 1919, Kilimanjaro, Behobeho, Nyangao, East Africa 1915–17

## Second World War

*Those in bold carried on the Queen's Colour*
**Dunkirk 1940**, North-West Europe 1940, Agordat, **Keren**, Syria 1941, Sidi Barrani, Djebel Tebaga, Peter's Corner, **North Africa 1940, 43**, Sangro, **Mozzagrogna**, Caldari, **Salerno**, St. Lucia, Battipaglia, Teano, Monte Camino, **Garigliano Crossing**, Damiano, **Anzio**, **Cassino II**, Ripa Ridge, Gabbiano, Advance to Florence, Monte Scalari, **Gothic Line**, **Coriano**, Croce, Casa Fortis, Savio Bridgehead, Valli di Commacchio, Senio, Argenta Gap, Italy 1943–45, Athens, Greece 1944–45

## Post-1945 (1st Battalion)

*Carried on the Regimental Colour*
**Korea 1952–53**

## Recipients of the Victoria Cross

Private (later Corporal) William Norman, 7th Regiment, Crimean War, 1854

Lieutenant Colonel Thomas Egerton Hale, 7th Regiment, Crimean War, 1855

Lieutenant (later Colonel) William Hope, 7th Regiment, Crimean War, 1855

Corporal Matthew Hughes, 7th Regiment, Crimean War, 1855

Captain Henry Mitchell Jones, 7th Regiment, Crimean War, 1855

Private Thomas Elsdon Ashford, 7th Regiment, Second Afghan War, 1880

Captain (later Brigadier) Charles Fitzclarence, 1st Battalion, Boer War, 1899

Lieutenant Maurice James Dease, 4th Battalion, First World War, 1914

Private Sidney Frank Godley, 4th Battalion, First World War, 1914

Lieutenant Wilbur Taylor Dartnell, 25th Battalion, First World War, 1915

The Reverend Edward Noel Mellish, Army Chaplains' Department (Royal Fusiliers), First World War, 1916

Captain Robert Gee, 2nd Battalion, First World War, 1917

Corporal George Jarratt, 8th Battalion, First World War, 1917

Sergeant John Molyneux, 2nd Battalion, First World War, 1917

Lance Sergeant (later 2nd Lieutenant) Frederick William Palmer, 22nd Battalion, First World War, 1917

Captain Walter Napleton Stone, 17th Battalion, First World War, 1917

Lieutenant Colonel Neville Bowes Elliott-Cooper, 8th Battalion, First World War, 1918

Lance Corporal (later Sergeant) Charles Graham Robertson, 10th Battalion, First World War, 1918

Sergeant Samuel George Pearse, 45th Battalion, North Russia Relief Force, 1919

Corporal Arthur Percy Sullivan, 45th Battalion, North Russia Relief Force, 1919

# The King's Regiment (Liverpool)

## 8th

One of only four British infantry regiments to have been associated with a city rather than a county, The King's Regiment was formed in 1685 by Lord Ferrers of Chartley as Princess Anne of Denmark's Regiment in honour of James II's daughter, the future Queen Anne. In 1716 it became The King's Regiment and was granted the privilege of wearing the White Horse of Hanover as its cap badge. It was numbered 8th (The King's Regiment) in 1751 and its first territorial attachment to Liverpool came in 1873. At the culmination of the Cardwell/Childers reforms it was given the title The King's (Liverpool Regiment) with two Regular battalions, two Militia battalions and seven Volunteer battalions, including the 7th Isle of Man Volunteers, the only military formation ever to represent that island. The regiment's first depot was at Peninsula Barracks in Warrington, still used today by the Territorial Army, and in 1911 it opened a sub-depot at Seaforth Barracks at Litherland in Liverpool. These closed in 1958 and were demolished to make way for residential housing but there is an amusing description of the depot in Robert Graves's wartime novel *Goodbye to All That* in which he and his brother officers try to imagine what would happen if the neighbouring explosives factory were to be blown up: 'Most of us held that the shock would immediately kill all the three thousand men of the camp besides destroying Litherland and a large part of Bootle.'

In no other episode in the regiment's history was the link with Liverpool more important than in the early days of the First World War. On 28 August 1914, in response to Lord Kitchener's urgent appeal for recruits, the Earl of Derby proposed the formation of special battalions which would recruit men from the same area or workplace in Liverpool: 'This should be a battalion of Pals, a battalion in which friends from the same office will fight shoulder to shoulder for the honour of Britain and the credit of Liverpool.' Within a week, thousands of Liverpudlians had volunteered to create the regiment's 17th, 18th, 19th and 20th Battalions which received the title 'City of Liverpool' but were better known as the 'Liverpool Pals'. Makeshift barracks for the 3,000 volunteers were created at an old watch factory in Prescot, in tents on Hooton Racecourse, in private houses near Sefton Park and ultimately in hastily constructed wooden huts in the grounds of Lord Derby's Knowsley Hall estate. In the following year it was announced that the four Liverpool Pals battalions would be deploying to the Western Front and excitement was high within the city. Among those leaving was Private W. B. Owens, who wrote to his parents summing up the feelings of many of the Liverpool Pals: 'Well we're away at last and 'tho no one feels that it's a solemn occasion to be in England for perhaps the last time, I think that the predominant feeling in every chap's heart – in mine at any rate – is one of pride and great content at being chosen to fight and endure for our dear ones and the old country.' Private Owens was killed in action on the first day of the Battle of the Somme, 1 July 1916.

The other great manifestation of Liverpool's support for the war was the regiment's 10th (Liverpool Scottish) Battalion which was formed of Scots living on Merseyside. With its headquarters in Fraser Street, which were built by public subscription, it had already seen service in the Boer War and its men wore Glengarry bonnets and kilts of Forbes tartan. It was also one of the first battalions of the Territorial Force to cross over to France and it went into action immediately on the Ypres Salient at the beginning of November 1914. One of the battalion's most famous soldiers was Captain Noel Chevasse RAMC, the doctor son of the Bishop of Liverpool, who was the only man to be awarded a double Victoria Cross during the First World War. Both he and his twin brother, Christopher, had taken part in the 1908 Olympic Games, competing in the 400 metres, and Chevasse Park in Liverpool's city centre is named in the family's honour. Another notable Liverpool man in the Liverpool Scottish was the actor Basil Rathbone, scion of the well-known Rathbone family (his uncle was Lord Mayor) and later famous for playing Sherlock Holmes in numerous films. At the end of the war the Liverpool Scottish became a Territorial battalion of Queen's Own Cameron Highlanders but the link with the city was not lost. The headquarters in Fraser Street were retained and were not demolished until 1967, when they made way for a car park, and in 1938 King George VI presented new Colours to the Battalion at a parade held in Liverpool at Goodison Park, the home of Everton Football Club.

Church service for 1st Battalion The King's Regiment (Liverpool) during the Boer War in 1900. In the latter stages of the conflict the battalion operated mainly in the Eastern Transvaal.

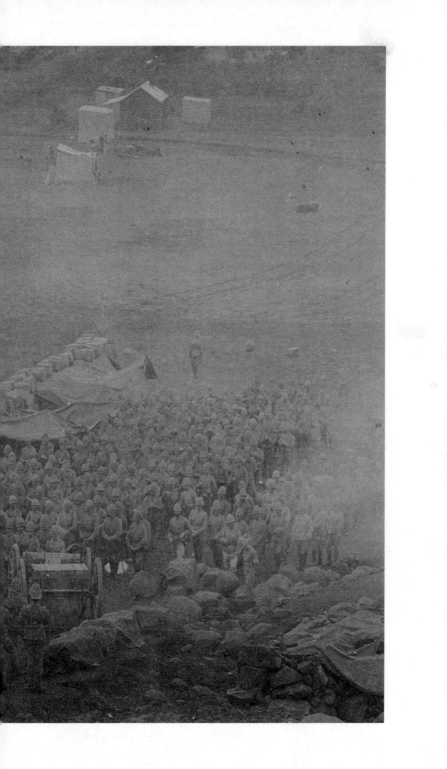

All told, the regiment raised forty-nine battalions for war service and twenty-nine of these served on all the main battlefronts; as a result casualties were disproportionally high – some 13,795 members of the regiment were killed in action during the war. Their sacrifice is commemorated by the imposing Liverpool cenotaph outside St George's Hall in the city centre, which was unveiled in November 1930. The long bronze reliefs on the memorial were sculpted by Herbert Tyson Smith; the panel facing St George's Hall depicts men marching off to war, while the one on the opposite, Lime Street, side commemorates those mourning the dead.

At the outbreak of the Second World War the regiment expanded once more, raising ten battalions, two of which served in the artillery and armoured roles. Both the 1st and the 13th Battalions served in Burma as Chindits, the remarkable long-range penetration force devised by Major General Orde Wingate for service behind Japanese lines. Before leaving for India, 13th King's had been employed on coastal defence duties and many of its men were either middle-aged or had low medical categories. Even so they responded to the challenge of operating in harsh jungle conditions against a vicious enemy and frequently proved their worth, as Private Leonard Grist from the Wirral explained in an interview for the Imperial War Museum. He and the rest of this platoon were making their way back towards India at the end of the operation when they encountered a large Japanese sentry:

He or it, I was never sure, literally screamed at us in broken English 'pigs you die', in the high staccato vocal chords singular to the Japanese. Reaching for a grenade, he had just managed to pull out the pin, when with great presence of mind Joe shot him through the forehead. With our minds now on the grenade, we both dived into the bushes either side of the track, sure enough the grenade exploded with a deafening crack, as we peered out we could see our Nip writhing and frothing from his big mouth, he was in his death throes. It was the first time I had ever witnessed a human being slowly leaving our world, he gave a convulsive shudder and rolled over face down into a heap, forever still. I could see a jagged hole the size of the boxers fist in the back of his head, what a mess a .303 bullet could make.

The memorial to the King's men who served as Chindits stands on the site of the former Harington Barracks in Formby, which served as the regimental depot and infantry training centre during the Second World War. It was demolished in the 1960s to make way for residential housing.

The regiment gained its last battle honour, 'Korea', for its service in 1952 and 1953 during which it fought at the Third Battle of the Hook, where Chinese and North Korean casualties were estimated at 1,050 killed and 800 wounded. Five years later The King's Regiment (Liverpool) amalgamated with The Manchester Regiment to form The King's Regiment; in 2006 this became the 2nd Battalion of The Duke of Lancaster's Regiment which adopted the King's old motto *Nec Aspera Terrant*, which may be translated freely as 'Difficulties be damned'. On amalgamation, the Colours of The King's Regiment (Liverpool) were laid up in Liverpool Cathedral.

Men of 7th Battalion The King's (Liverpool) Regiment in a front line post near La Bassée, 15 March 1918.

# Battle Honours

## Pre-1914

*Carried on the Regimental Colour*
**Blenheim, Ramillies, Oudenarde, Malplaquet, Dettingen, Martinique 1809, Niagara, Delhi 1857, Lucknow, Peiwar Kotal, Afghanistan 1878–80, Burma 1885–87, Defence of Ladysmith, South Africa 1899–1902**

## First World War (49 battalions)

*Those in bold carried on the Queen's Colour*
Mons, **Retreat from Mons, Marne 1914, Aisne 1914, Ypres 1914, 15, 17,** Langemarck 1914, 17, Gheluvelt, Nonne Boschen, Neuve Chapelle, Gravenstafel, St Julien, Frezenberg, Bellewaarde, Aubers, **Festubert 1915, Loos, Somme 1916, 18,** Albert 1916, 18, Bazentin, Deville Wood, Guillemont, Ginchy, Flers-Courcelette, Morval, Le Transloy, Ancre 1916, Bapaume 1917, 18, **Arras 1917, 18, Scarpe 1917, 18,** Arleux, Pilckem, Menin Road, Polygon Wood, Poelcappelle, Passchendaele, **Cambrai 1917, 18,** St. Quentin, Rosières, Avre, Lys, Estaires, Messines 1918, Bailleul, Kemmel, Bethune, Scherpenberg, Drocourt-Queant, Hindenburg Line, Epehy, Canal du Nord, St Quentin Canal, Selle, Sambre, France and Flanders 1914–18, Doiran 1917, Macedonia 1915–18, N.W. Frontier, India 1915, Archangel 1918–19

## Post-1918

*Carried on the Regimental Colour*
**Afghanistan 1919**

The King's Regiment (Liverpool)

## Second World War

*Those in bold carried on the Queen's Colour*
**Normandy Landing.** North-West Europe 1944, **Cassino II, Trasimene Line, Tuori, Capture of Forli, Rimini Line,** Italy 1944–45, **Athens,** Greece 1944–45, **Chindits 1943, Chindits 1944,** Burma 1943–44

## Post-1945 (1st Battalion)

*Carried on the Regimental Colour*
**The Hook 1953, Korea 1952–53**

## Recipients of the Victoria Cross

Sergeant Harry Hampton, 2nd Battalion, Boer War, 1900

Corporal (later Captain) Henry James Knight, 1st Battalion, Boer War, 1900

Private (later Sergeant) William Edward Heaton 1st Battalion, Boer War, 1900

Lance Corporal Joseph Harcourt Tombs, 1st Battalion, First World War, 1915

2nd Lieutenant Edward Felix Baxter, 1/8th Battalion, First World War, 1916

Private Arthur Herbert Procter, 1/5th Battalion, First World War, 1916

Sergeant David Jones, 12th Battalion, First World War, 1916

Captain Oswald Austin Reid, 2nd Battalion, First World War, 1917

Private (later Corporal) Jack Thomas Counter, 1st Battalion, First World War, 1918

# The Royal Norfolk Regiment

## 9th

One of the most mysterious incidents in the history of the British Army occurred on the late afternoon of 12 August 1915 when 1/5th Norfolk Regiment went into the attack against Turkish positions on the Gallipoli peninsula near Suvla Bay. In their ranks was C Company, the so-called 'Sandringham Company', which was composed of men who worked on the royal estate at Sandringham House and were part-time volunteers of the Territorial Force. Their company commander was Captain Francis Beck, land agent to the estate; the estate's foremen, butlers, head gamekeepers and head gardeners were the NCOs; the farm labourers, grooms and household servants made up the rank and file. The Norfolks were on the right of the British line and seem to have advanced quickly and confidently towards the enemy positions. At the end of the attack, which failed to take its objectives, most of the survivors made it back to their own lines but sixteen officers and 250 other ranks from the 1/5th Battalion disappeared and, according to the official despatch, 'Nothing more was ever seen or heard of any of them. They charged into the forest and were lost to sight or sound. Not one of them ever came back.' It was not until four years later that the remains were found scattered over a wide area near the original Turkish lines, but even then doubts remained as to the fate of the Sandringham Company. Rumours abounded that survivors of the attack had been summarily executed by the Turks and an even stranger story emerged when two New Zealand veterans claimed that they had seen the Norfolks march into a mysterious cloud that first engulfed them then lifted and drifted away, leaving nobody behind. After the war George V unveiled a memorial within the grounds of Sandringham church dedicated to the seventy-seven local dead of the First World War; there is also a memorial plaque on the right of the lych-gate of the church of St Peter & St Paul in West Newton. In 1999 the BBC screened a drama based on the Sandringham Company. Entitled *All the King's Men*; it starred David Jason as Captain Frank Beck.

Although the losses at Suvla Bay were relatively small compared to the regiment's overall wartime casualty list of 5,576, and while it was only a small part of the Norfolks' war history, the incident typified the regiment's sense of itself. It emphasised its connection to the Royal Family – long after the war Queen Alexandra continued to take a special interest in the fate of the Sandringham Company – and it underlined the close association that existed between the regiment and the county of Norfolk, one that went back to 1782 when the 9th Foot was designated the East Norfolk Regiment. Between 1885 and 1887 Britannia Barracks in Norwich was constructed as the regiment's depot, taking its name from the figure of Britannia on the regiment's cap badge, an honour awarded by Queen Anne in recognition of the regiment's gallantry during the Battle of Almansa in 1707. Britannia also provided the Norfolks

HRH Prince Edward, Prince of Wales, wearing civilian clothes, inspects 4th Battalion The Norfolk Regiment during a visit to Norwich on 30 May 1928.

with their nickname 'The Holy Boys' after Spanish soldiers mistook it for a representation of the Virgin Mary during the Peninsular War. It also gave rise to a well-worn army joke that the Norfolks were the only regiment allowed to have a woman in barracks. Britannia Barracks was later incorporated into the modern buildings of HM Prison Norwich and the regimental museum was transferred to the Shire Hall, also in Norwich.

In 1940, during the Second World War, the regiment was the victim of a war crime perpetrated by a Waffen SS unit. It took place on 27 May in the village of Le Paradis, close to the La Bassée canal, where a force comprising 2nd Royal Norfolk Regiment and 1st Royal Scots was attempting to slow down the German advance as the British Expeditionary Force retreated towards the beaches at Dunkirk. A party of ninety-nine men of the Norfolks became isolated in the farmhouse at Le Paradis and when their ammunition ran out their commander, Major Lisle Ryder, ordered them to surrender to 4th Company, SS Division Totenkopf, under the command of Hauptsturm-führer Fritz Knöchlein. The captured men were marched to a nearby barn where they were executed by two German machine-gunners. Survivors were then bayoneted but amidst the carnage two men managed to escape death. One of them was Private William O'Callaghan and the other Private Albert Pooley, who later described what had happened to him: 'Men fell like grass before a scythe … I felt a searing pain and pitched forward … my scream of pain mingled with the cries of my mates, but even before I fell into the heap of dying men, the thought stabbed my brain "If I ever get out of here, the swine that did this will pay for it."' After the war Knöchlein was arrested for his role in the war crime and was executed in Hamburg in January 1949.

During the Second World War five members of the Royal Norfolk Regiment received the Victoria Cross for conspicuous gallantry. Two were awarded as a result of action in Burma – Captain John Niel Randle at the Battle of Kohima in April 1944 and Lieutenant George Arthur Knowland at Kangaw in January 1945. The other three were awarded in France – to Company Sergeant Major George Gristock on the River Escaut during the retreat to Dunkirk; Corporal Sidney Bates, who died of his wounds while manning a machine-gun position in Normandy in August 1944; and Major David Jamieson, a company commander in the 7th Battalion, who held a bridgehead over the River Orne under heavy fire during fighting in Normandy. The son of the then chairman of Vickers Armstrong, Jamieson had joined up as a private soldier in the Territorial Army and chose the Norfolks because his family had a holiday home in the county. Standing six feet five inches, he was one of the tallest men in the regiment and later in life was designated ceremonial 'umbrella man' to Queen Elizabeth The Queen Mother, holding an umbrella over Her Majesty at social functions when it was raining.

After the end of the Second World War the Norfolks were one of sixteen British infantry regiments that saw action in the Korean War (1950–53). It was a hard and bitter conflict with much of the fighting taking place in conditions not so very different from the Western Front forty years earlier. Many of the soldiers in 1st Royal Norfolks were National Servicemen often bewildered at finding themselves fighting so far from home in a remote

Men of the 1st Battalion Royal Norfolk Regiment leave for service in Korea on 30 August 1951. It spent 10 months on the front line, improving line defences with barbed wire and trench systems and sending out patrols. During the tour the battalion lost 33 officers and men killed in action and 108 injured.

part of the world of which they had very little knowledge. One of them was Bob Walding, who later recorded his memories for the Norfolks' regimental museum: 'Nobody told us what the war was about. We just picked it up as we went along. To be honest, when I went out there I didn't know if I was fighting for the North or South; it was as bad as that ...'

Earlier, in 1935, the regiment had received a royal title, becoming The Royal Norfolk Regiment, but it was a comparatively short-lived honour. Twenty-four years later The Royal Norfolk Regiment joined forces with its close neighbours, The Suffolk Regiment, to become 1st East Anglian Regiment; this in turn became part of The Royal Anglian Regiment in 1964. A link with the past was maintained when A Company of the new regiment's 1st Battalion was designated the Royal Norfolk Company.

## Battle Honours

### Pre-1914

*Carried on the Regimental Colour*
Belleisle, Havannah, Martinque 1794, Rolica, Vimiera, Corunna, Busaco, Salamanca, Vittoria, San Sebastián, Nive, Peninsula, Cabool 1842, Moodkee, Ferozeshah, Sobraon, Sevastopol, Kabul 1879, Afghanistan 1879–80, Paardeberg, South Africa 1900–02

## First World War (19 battalions)

*Those in bold carried on the Queen's Colour*
**Mons**, **Le Cateau**, Retreat from Mons, **Marne 1914**, Aisne
1914, La Bassée 1914, **Ypres 1914, 15, 17, 18**, Gravenstafel,
St. Julien, Frezenberg, Bellewaarde, Loos, **Somme 1916, 18**,
Albert 1916, 18, Delville Wood, Pozières, Guillemont, Flers-
Courcelette, Morval, Thiepval, Le Transloy, Ancre Heights,
Ancre 1916, 18, Arras 1917, Vimy 1917, Scarpe 1917,
Arleux, Oppy, Pilckem, Langemarck 1917, Polygon Wood,
Broodseinde, Poelcappelle, Passchendaele, Cambrai 1917, 18,
St. Quentin, Bapaume 1918, Lys, Bailleul, Kemmel,
Scherpenberg, Amiens, **Hindenburg Line**, Épéhy, Canal du
Nord, St. Quentin Canal, Beaurevoir, Selle, Sambre, France
and Flanders 1914–18, Italy 1917–18, Suvla, **Landing at
Suvla**, Scimitar Hill, Gallipoli 1915, Egypt 1915–17, **Gaza**,
El Mughar, Nebi Samwil, Jerusalem, Jaffa, Tell 'Asur,
Megiddo, Sharon, Palestine 1917–18, **Shaiba, Kut al Amara
1915, 17**, Ctesiphon, Defence of Kut al Amara, Mesopotamia
1914–18

## Second World War

*Those in bold carried on the Queen's Colour*
Defence of Escaut, **St Omer-La bassee**, St Valery-en-Caux,
**Normandy Landing**, Caen, Le Perier Ridge, **Brieux
Bridgehead, Venraij, Rhineland**, Hochwld, Lingen, Brinkum,
**North-West Europe 1940, 44–45**, Johore, Muar, Batu Pahat,
**Singapore Island**, Malaya 1942, **Kohima, Aradura**, Mandalay,
**Burma 1944–45**

## Post-1945 (1st Battalion)

*Carried on the Regimental Colour*
**Korea 1951–52**

## Recipients of the Victoria Cross

Acting Lieutenant Colonel John Sherwood-Kelly, The Norfolk
Regiment commanding 1st Royal Inniskilling Fusiliers, First
World War, 1917

Company Sergeant Major George Gristock, 2nd Battalion,
Second World War, 1940

Captain John Niel Randle, 2nd Battalion, Second World
War, 1944

Corporal Sidney Bates, 1st Battalion, Second World War, 1944

Captain David Auldjo Jamieson, 5th Battalion, Second World
War, 1944

Lieutenant George Arthur Knowland, The Royal Norfolk
Regiment attached No. 1 Commando, Second World
War, 1945

# The Royal Lincolnshire Regiment

## 10th

Always known as 'The Poachers', The Royal Lincolnshire Regiment was the epitome of a thoroughly decent English county regiment – unassuming, solid and intensely proud of its long history and traditions. It took the nickname from the regimental quick march 'The Lincolnshire Poacher', which itself is one of England's best-known and best-loved folk songs, rightly regarded as an unofficial anthem for Lincolnshire, the county that supplied the regiment with the bulk of its recruits. The regimental museum is housed in Lincoln's City Barracks, built in 1857 for the Loyal North Lincoln Militia, and now the Museum for Lincolnshire Life. The Lincolnshire Regiment started life in 1685 as Granville's Regiment of Foot, named after its first Colonel, John Granville, 1st Earl of Bath, a Privy Councillor and a Royalist supporter in the civil war of 1642–49. In 1751 it became the 10th Foot and thirty years later it was accorded the territorial title of North Lincolnshire. In common with most infantry regiments of that period it recruited heavily in Ireland and the regiment was present at the action at Carrickfergus in February 1760 which thwarted an attempted French invasion during the Seven Years War.

In the aftermath the regiment spent most of its life abroad, fighting in North America during the War of Independence and in the Peninsula during the war against Napoleon. From these experiences came the memoirs of Jeremy Lister, who was born at Shibden Hall, near Halifax in West Yorkshire, and who joined the regiment as an ensign in 1770. He was present at Lexington at the outbreak of hostilities and his narrative of events pulls no punches in its descriptions of the brutality of some of the early battles. On coming across bodies of the men of his regiment killed at Concord Bridge, Lister found that they had been 'afterwards scalp'd their Eyes goug'd their Noses and Ears cut off, such barbarity exercis'd upon the Corps could scarcely be paralelld [sic] by the most uncivilised Savages'. With its unflinching descriptions of British ineptitude, Lister's narrative enjoyed considerable success and in 2003 inspired the equally successful silent comedy art house film *The Deserter*, which follows the mis-adventures of a drummer in the 10th Foot during the war.

In the middle of the nineteenth century the regiment spent several years in India and saw action in the First Sikh War, where it won the battle honour 'Sobraon' for its role in taking part in the defeat of a Sikh army 30,000-strong in the Punjab. During the fighting in the Sikh entrenchments at Sobraon the 10th joined forces with the 29th Foot, later The Worcestershire Regiment, and the camaraderie forged in the bloody close-quarter fighting led to the introduction of a custom whereby officers and sergeants of both regiments addressed each other thereafter as 'My Dear Cousin'. When new barracks and a depot were opened in Lincoln for the regiment in the late 1870s they were named after the battle and most

Enniskillen in County Fermanagh, 1923: a group of soldiers from 1st Battalion The Lincolnshire Regiment pose for a formal photograph with three of their officers.

of the buildings and the impressive brick-built keep of Sobraon Barracks are still in existence as a centre for Territorial Army and Cadet forces.

Perhaps the most unusual deployment came in 1868 when the regiment spent three years in Japan guarding the international district in Yokohama. A relatively undemanding assignment, it none the less changed the life of the bandmaster John William Fenton, born in Kinsale, Ireland. One day a group of Japanese naval cadets heard the band practising and were so impressed that they persuaded their superiors to invite Fenton to become their instructor. Brass instruments were duly ordered from London and Japan's first naval band was formed. Two years later Fenton added to his laurels by writing the music for the original version of Japan's national anthem 'Kimi ga Yo' with words from a tenth-century poem. When the 10th Foot returned to Britain in 1871, Fenton stayed on in Japan for a further six years, first as a naval bandmaster and then as the bandmaster of the Imperial Court. After their return the 10th Foot became The Lincolnshire Regiment with two Regular battalions and one Militia battalion.

The outbreak of the First World War posed several challenges to the Lincolns, which, like every other regiment in the country, had to increase its manpower. Although a large county, Lincolnshire is not heavily populated, yet the regiment still managed to raise thirteen battalions in addition to its two Regular battalions. One of the more unusual sources of recruits was the island of Bermuda where the 2nd Battalion was based before the outbreak of hostilities. In December 1914 a contingent of volunteers from the Bermuda Volunteer Rifle Corps arrived in England and served with the Lincolns on the Western Front as the first colonial volunteer unit. The connection is still maintained by the succeeding regiments, The Royal Anglians and The Bermuda Regiment.

The other noteworthy battalion was The 10th Lincolnshire Regiment, the 'Grimsby Chums', the only 'pals' battalion to be given a different title. It was raised in Grimsby from a nucleus of 250 boys at Wintringham Grammar School and the idea spread to other neighbouring towns in north-east Lincolnshire, among them Boston, Louth and Scunthorpe, so that a complete battalion of more than a thousand Lincolnshire men was quickly raised to serve in 34th Division. The Grimsby Chums undertook their training on Lord Yarborough's estate at Brocklesbury and marched off to war full of hope and excitement, anxious to see action. Their wish was granted on 1 July 1916, the first day of the Somme, when they attacked the village of La Boisselle following the explosion of a huge mine known as Lochnagar. However, the attack quickly became bogged down in heavy German machine-gun fire and many of the Grimsby Chums found themselves trapped in the mine crater, the largest on the Western Front and to this day a place of pilgrimage. In total the Grimsby Chums suffered 502 casualties that day – fifteen officers and 487 other ranks. According to a contemporary newspaper report, when the news reached Grimsby a week later hardly a street in the port was left unaffected by the tragedy and most houses had their blinds drawn in mourning. John Barker, the last of the survivors of the Grimsby Chums, died in 1995 aged 101 and there is a memorial to the battalion in St James's Church, Grimsby.

Wellington Barracks, London, 16 August 1929: men of 1st Battalion
The Lincolnshire Regiment rehearse to mount the King's Guard at
Buckingham Palace. These duties are normally performed by a Foot
Guards battalion.

Thankfully the pals concept was not tested again in the Second World War but The Lincolnshire Regiment still played a full part in the conflict. The regiment's two Territorial Army battalions, 4th and 6th, were mobilised immediately on the outbreak of war and the latter was sent to France together with the Regular 2nd Battalion. Both were evacuated after the retreat to Dunkirk in May 1940. Subsequently the 2nd and the 4th Battalions served in North-West Europe 1944–45 while the 6th Battalion served in North Africa and Italy and the 1st Battalion saw service in Burma on the Arakan front. During the fighting in the Ngakyedauk Pass in February 1944, Acting Major Charles Ferguson Hoey MC attacked a Japanese machine-gun position and silenced it despite being mortally wounded. For his outstanding courage he won the Victoria Cross, one of eight awarded to the regiment.

After the Second World War the regiment was granted a royal title, becoming The Royal Lincolnshire Regiment, but it was a relatively brief accolade. In 1960 it amalgamated with The Northamptonshire Regiment to become the 2nd Battalion of the newly formed East Anglian Regiment (Duchess of Gloucester's Own Royal Lincolnshire and Northamptonshire) but that too was short-lived, for in 1964 it became the 2nd Battalion The Royal Anglian Regiment. To maintain the links with the past the battalion retains the nickname 'The Poachers' and A Company is the Royal Lincolnshire Company. On losing its separate identity, the Colours of The Royal Lincolnshire Regiment were laid up in Lincoln Cathedral.

# Battle Honours

## Pre-1914

*Carried on the Regimental Colour*
Steenkirk, Blenheim, Ramillies, Oudenarde, Malplaquet,
Bouchain, Lexington, Bunker's Hill, Peninsula, Sobraon,
Mooltan, Goojuarat, Punjab, Lucknow, Atbara, Khartoum,
Paardeberg, South Africa 1900–02

## First World War (19 battalions)

*Those in bold carried on the Queen's Colour*
**Mons**, Le Cateau, Retreat from Mons, **Marne 1914**, Aisne
1914, 18, La Bassée 1914, **Messines 1914, 17, 18**, Armentières
1914 **Ypres 1914, 15, 17**, Nonne Bosschen, **Neuve Chapelle**,
Gravenstafel, St. Julien, Frezenberg, Bellewaarde, Aubers,
**Loos, Somme 1916, 18**, Albert 1916, 18, Bazentin, Delville
Wood, Pozières, Flers-Courcelette, Morval, Thiepval, Ancre
1916, 18, Arras 1917, 18, Scarpe 1917, 18, Arleux, Pilckem,
Langemarck 1917, Menin Road, Polygon Wood, Broodseinde,
Poelcappelle, Passchendaele, Cambrai 1917, 18, St. Quentin,
Bapaume 1918, **Lys**, Estaires, Bailleul, Kemmel, Amiens,
Drocourt Quéant, **Hindenburg Line**, Épéhy, Canal du Nord,
St. Quentin Canal, Beaurevoir, Selle, Sambre, France and
Flanders 1914–18, **Suvla**, Landing at Suvla, Scimitar Hill,
Gallipoli 1915, Egypt 1916

## Second World War

*Those in bold carried on the Queen's Colour*
Vist, Norway 1940, **Dunkirk 1940, Normandy Landing**,
Cambes, **Fontenay le Pesnil**, Defence of Rauray, Caen, Orne,
Bourguébus Ridge, Troarn, Nederrijn, Le Havre, **Antwerp-
Turnhout Canal**, Venraij, Venlo Pocket, **Rhineland**, Hochwald,
Lingen, Bremen, Arnhem 1945, North-West Europe 1940,

1944–45, Sedjenane I, Mine de Sedjenane, Argoub Selah, **North Africa 1943, Salerno,** Vietri Pass, Capture of Naples, Cava di Terreni, Volturno Crossing, Garigliano Crossing, Monte Tuga, **Gothic Line,** Monte Gridolfo, Gemmano Ridge, Lamone Crossing, San Marino, Italy 1943–45, Donbaik, Point 201 (Arakan), North Arakan, Buthidaung, **Ngakyedauk Pass,** Ramree, **Burma 1943–45**

## Recipients of the Victoria Cross

Private Denis Dempsey, 10th Regiment, Indian Mutiny, 1857
Private John Kirk, 10th Regiment, Indian Mutiny, 1857
Lieutenant (later Lieutenant General Sir) Henry Marshman
    Havelock-Allan, 10th Regiment, Indian Mutiny, 1857
Captain (later Brigadier) Percy Howard Hansen,
    6th Battalion, First World War, 1915
Corporal Charles Richard Sharpe, 2nd Battalion, First World
    War, 1915
Corporal (later Sergeant) Arthur Evans, 6th Battalion,
    First World War, 1918
Major Charles Ferguson Hoey, 1st Battalion, Second World
    War, 1944
Captain John Henry Cound Brunt, The Sherwood Foresters,
    attached 6th Lincolnshire Regiment, Second World
    War, 1944

# The Devonshire Regiment

## 11th

Driving along the main road from Fricourt to Maricourt across the Somme battlefield – the D938 Albert–Péronne road – you pass the old British front lines where the British 7th Division went into the attack in the early hours of 1 July 1916, the first day of the great battle. It is one of the many hallowed spots on the Somme where thousands of British soldiers died miles from home, but in this case it is a site that is for ever a part of England's West Country. Just before the village of Mametz, in a small wood known as Mansel Copse, stands a monument to the men of 8th Devonshire Regiment and 9th Devonshire Regiment who were part of the first wave of British attacks on that fateful morning. Of their number 161 did not return; they were killed by enfilading German machine-gunners whose position by the church in Mametz had not been destroyed during the earlier artillery bombardment, even though its dangers had been pointed out by one of the Devons' officers, Captain D. L. Martin. To make his point he had even constructed a plasticine model of the area to show the threat posed by the German machine-gun position, but this had been ignored.

Three days later, after the fighting had died down and the enemy positions had eventually been taken, the

Heyday of Empire: 2nd Battalion The Devonshire Regiment march out of Fort William in Calcutta. Built on the eastern banks of the River Hooghly it was the centre of British military power in Bengal and is still a military base, being the headquarters of the Indian Army's Eastern Command.

Devons returned and buried their dead in the old front line trench from which they had launched the assault. Above it a simple wooden cross was placed with the noble words: 'The Devonshires held this Trench: The Devonshires hold it still'. Although the cross disappeared long ago, in the 1980s a handsome stone memorial was placed beside the cemetery gate with the same words contained within a depiction of the original cross. Among those killed that day was Lieutenant William Noel Hodgson MC, son of the Bishop of St Edmundsbury and Ipswich and a noted war poet whose final poem, 'Before Action', was grimly prophetic, the last line reading 'Help me to die, O Lord'.

The regiment came into being as the Duke of Beaufort's Musketeers in 1685, raised to defend Bristol against the Duke of Monmouth's unsuccessful attempt to seize the throne from James II, although the records also show that it had an earlier life as the Marquess of Worcester's Regiment of Foot, which existed for a few brief months in 1667. In 1751 it was numbered the 11th Foot and in 1782 it received the territorial designation North Devonshire. The final cementing of the county connection came in 1881 when it merged with the Devon Militia and was given the title The Devonshire Regiment with its depot at Topsham Barracks, Exeter. Later this became Wyvern Barracks and it is still in existence as a Territorial Army facility.

By that time the regiment had acquired a substantial war record, having served under the Duke of Marlborough during the War of the Spanish Succession (1701–14) and under the Duke of Cumberland at the battles of Dettingen (1743) and Fontenoy (1745) during the War of the

Austrian Succession. It had also engaged Jacobite forces twice – at Sheriffmuir during the 1715 rebellion and at Glen Shiel in 1719 when its grenadier company played a leading role under the command of Major Milburn. The latter battle site is today under the protection of the National Trust for Scotland and the walled enclosure which formed the Jacobites' ammunition store is still visible. In the wars against Revolutionary France, the 11th North Devonshire Regiment had the distinction of serving as marines or 'sea-soldiers' during the naval battle of Cape St Vincent where a British fleet under Admiral Sir John Jervis defeated a larger Spanish fleet commanded by Admiral Don José de Córdoba y Ramos on 14 February 1797. It was also in action in the Peninsula where it was given the nickname 'The Bloody Eleventh'.

From the outset the Devons built a reputation as doughty fighters who enjoyed the trust of those who commanded them and quickly won their respect. In 1899 at the outset of the Boer War, 1st Devons was one of the experienced battalions sent out to bolster the British forces and on 21 October was in action at Elandslaagte in the company of two other equally fine battalions – 1st Manchester Regiment and 2nd Gordon Highlanders. The Devons were the first to go into the attack, streaming forward across the veldt, the men firing controlled volleys, the company commanders blowing whistles. Just short of the Boer positions they regrouped to wait for the Gordons, a scene later described by Drummer Ernest Boulden of D Company in an ungrammatical but heartfelt letter to his parents: '... and then we had to lie down flat and the Bullits came round us quite thick and we hadvanced in such a splendid order they [Boers] said they were sirprised to see it and we said we hadvanced like a stone wall, and so we did ...'

A cavalry charge finished the battle, which was one of the only clear-cut tactical successes during the war. In the subsequent fighting at Wagon Hill near Ladysmith the regiment won its first Victoria Cross, awarded to Lieutenant James Edward Ignatius Masterson for exceptional bravery on 6 January 1900. A thirty-seven-year-old Irishman who had been commissioned from the ranks, Masterson demonstrated 'unselfish heroism' in taking an urgent message to the Imperial Light Horse detachment, showing no regard for his own safety while under heavy enemy fire. He survived the war and retired from the army in 1912. By coincidence, one of his ancestors had shown similar courage during the Napoleonic Wars by capturing a French eagle during the Battle of Barossa in 1811. The incident is described in Bernard Cornwell's novel *Sharpe's Fury*.

At the beginning of 1900 the Devons' 2nd Battalion joined the war and quickly distinguished itself in the fighting in Natal where the men caught the eye of their brigade commander, Colonel Walter Kitchener, the younger brother of General Lord Herbert Kitchener, the army's chief of staff. Later he repaid that debt by writing the following encomium in the regimental war history: 'No one can quite appreciatively follow the story of the work of the Devons, unless he realises the intense feeling of comradeship that animates these West-country men. To work with Devonshire men is to realise in the flesh theintensity of the local county loyalty so graphically depicted by Charles Kingsley in his *Westward Ho!* and other novels.'

In 1953, 1st Battalion The Devonshire Regiment was posted to Kenya for a three-year tour at the height of the Mau-Mau insurgency, also known as the Kenyan Emergency. Once in Kenya, serge battledress was exchanged for khaki drill uniforms.

During the Second World War the Devons added to the West Country's military reputation by fighting on all the main battlefronts, while the 12th Battalion distinguished itself by serving in Europe as part of 6th Airlanding Brigade which went into battle by glider during the Normandy landings. In 1948 the regiment lost its 2nd Battalion and ten years later it amalgamated with the neighbouring Dorset Regiment (39th/54th) to form The Devonshire and Dorset Regiment, which in turn became part of The Rifles in 2007. One of the Devon and Dorsets' most distinguished soldiers was Lieutenant Colonel H. [erbert] Jones who transferred to The Parachute Regiment in 1979 and was awarded the Victoria Cross during the Falklands War of 1982. There is a plaque to his memory in the Church of St Thomas of Canterbury in Kingswear, Devon, where Jones spent part of his childhood.

On amalgamation the Colours of The Devonshire Regiment were laid up in Exeter Cathedral and the regimental records are held in Dorset at The Keep Military Museum, Bridport Road, Dorchester.

---

## Battle Honours

### Pre-1914

*Carried on the Regimental Colour*
**Dettingen, Salamanca, Pyrenees, Nivelle, Nive, Orthes, Toulouse, Peninsula, Afghanistan 1879–80, Tirah, Defence of Ladysmith, Relief of Ladysmith, South Africa 1899–1902**

### First World War (25 battalions)

*Those in bold are carried on the Queen's Colour*
Aisne 1914, 18, **La Bassée 1914**, Armentières 1914, Neuve Chapelle, Hill 60, **Ypres 1915, 17**, Gravenstafel, St. Julien, Frezenberg, Aubers, **Loos, Somme 1916, 18**, Albert 1916, Bazentin, Delville Wood, Guillemont, Flers-Courcelette, Morval, Arras 1917, 18, Vimy 1917, Scarpe 1917, Bullecourt, Pilckem, Langemarck 1917, Polygon Wood, Broodseinde, Poelcappelle, Passchendaele, Rosières, Villers Bretonneux, Lys, Hazebrouck, **Bois des Buttes**, Marne 1918, Tardenois, Bapaume 1918, **Hindenburg Line**, Havrincourt, Épéhy, Canal du Nord, Beaurevoir, Cambrai 1918, Selle, Sambre, France and Flanders 1914–18, Piave, **Vittorio Veneto**, Italy 1917–18, **Doiran 1917, 18**, Macedonia 1915–18, Egypt 1916–17, Gaza,

Nebi Samwil, Jerusalem, Tel Asur, **Palestine 1917–18**, Tigris 1916, Kut al Amara 1917, **Mesopotamia 1916–18**

## Second World War

*Those in bold are carried on the Queen's Colour*
**Normandy Landing,** Port en Bessin, Tilly sur Seulles, Caen, St. Pierre la Vielle, Nederrijn, Roer, **Rhine,** Ibbenburen, **North-West Europe 1944–45, Landing in Sicily, Regalbuto,** Sicily 1943, Landing at Porto San Venere, Italy 1943, **Malta 1940–42, Imphal,** Shenam Pass, Tamu Road, Ukhrul, **Myinmu Bridgehead,** Kyaukse 1945, **Burma 1943–45**

## Recipients of the Victoria Cross

Lieutenant (later Major) James Edward Ignatius Masterson, 1st Battalion, Boer War, 1900

Private (later Corporal) Theodore Veale, 8th Battalion, First World War, 1916

Lance Corporal (later Captain) George Onions, 1st Battalion, First World War, 1918

# The Somerset Light Infantry (Prince Albert's)

## 13th

For many years, India, the 'Jewel in the Crown', was a second home for the British Army. During the period of the British Raj, which lasted from the end of the Indian Mutiny in 1857 to independence in 1947, when the subcontinent was partitioned and the new state of Pakistan came into being, hundreds of thousands of British soldiers served in India as part of the resident garrison. It was fitting therefore that the last British infantry regiment to leave India should be 1st Battalion The Somerset Light Infantry, which was not only one of the oldest regiments in the British Army but could look back on a long history of service on the subcontinent. On 28 February 1948, under the command of Lieutenant Colonel John Platt, who had joined the Somersets in 1926, the battalion paraded for the last time in India, marching proudly on to the Apollo Bunder in Bombay before embarking on the troopship SS *Empress of Australia* which lay offshore in the Bombay roads. It was an impressive occasion with the Colour Party marching on to the Regimental March played by the band of the Royal Indian Engineers while guards from other Indian regiments and the Royal Indian Navy stood smartly to attention. Speeches were made and Platt was presented

The Colour Party of 1st Battalion The Somerset Light Infantry marches down the steps of the Apollo Bunder in Bombay on 28 February 1948, before embarking on the troopship *Empress of Australia*. They were the last troops to leave newly independent India.

with a large silver model of the Gateway of India, the huge triumphal arch which dominates Bombay's harbour area.

Then it was all over. To the strains of 'Auld Lang Syne' the escorts trooped the Colours down the centre of the parade and through the Gateway of India to the waiting launches. Above them, still in their positions, the bands of the Indian Army continued to play 'Auld Lang Syne': incongruously, the chorus was taken up by thousands of Indian voices as the *Empress of Australia* slipped her anchor and headed for the open sea. After 126 years The Somerset Light Infantry was finally coming home. When the battalion arrived back at Jellalabad Barracks, the depot in Taunton, the welcome was equally enthusiastic as the people of Somerset hailed their local regiment. Built between 1879 and 1881, Jellalabad Barracks remained in existence until the 1980s when much of it was demolished. Only the brick-built keep remains behind the open spaces of Vivary Park on land that was formerly a medieval fish farm, or *vivarium*, for nearby Taunton Priory and Taunton Castle.

Whatever else the passing of time has done to the old barrack buildings it cannot efface the memory of the long historical relationship that grew up between Somerset and Jalalabad, the second largest city in eastern Afghanistan, not far from the border with Pakistan. The walled city has been central to the history of The Somerset Light Infantry since 1822 when it was designated a Light Infantry regiment – by that stage the regiment had been numbered 13th and given the territorial designation of Somersetshire. That same year it moved to Chatham in preparation for a twenty-three-year-long deployment to

India. It arrived in Calcutta in the summer of 1823 but was quickly embroiled in fighting in neighbouring Burma where it came under the command of Lieutenant Colonel (later General Sir) Robert Sale, a veteran of Seringapatam, a ferocious disciplinarian but loved by his men for his courage in leading from the front. The conflict, which came to be known as the First Anglo-Burmese War, culminated with the capture of Rangoon in 1826 in which the 13th played a leading role.

At the conclusion of hostilities the regiment returned to garrison duty in India, but before long they were in action again and once more under Sale's command. In the winter of 1839 the British sent an army into Afghanistan to remove Amir Dost Mohammed and to replace him with a British puppet ruler. Sale commanded the 1st Bengal Brigade, which included the 13th, and the force quickly marched into Kandahar without meeting any significant resistance. The regiment took part in the Battle of Ghazni in July 1839, which allowed Shah Shujah to be installed as Afghanistan's ruler, but the victory was not decisive; forces loyal to Dost Mohammed regrouped and in 1841 the British were obliged to withdraw. Under Sale's command the 13th made its way to the fortified town of Jalalabad, which was put under siege. To encourage other survivors from the retreat to join them the 13th flew their Colours from the ramparts as a sign that they were still holding out and were prepared to resist. Sale's wife Florentia was no less thick skinned: the soldiers called her 'the grenadier in petticoats' and at one stage she taunted her husband's men for running away 'like a flock of sheep with a wolf at their heels'. After five months of inaction Sale decided to break out: he took the

Princess Margaret Rose inspects a guard of honour of the
4th Battalion Somerset Light Infantry at the Bath Festival on
1 May 1948.

fight to the besieging forces, which quickly disengaged and fled to Kabul.

The defence of Jalalabad was the making of the men of the 13th Somersetshire Light Infantry, which returned to India as the heroes of the hour, the only regiment to give a good account of itself and to survive in what had been a disastrous setback for the British and Indian armies. In a letter to his parents, Ensign C. G. C. Stapleton reported that 'every regiment in Hindustan shall on our march down, turn out and present arms to us in review order'. Back in London, Queen Victoria was so impressed that she ordered that the regiment should bear the additional title 'Prince Albert's' and to honour its courage in Afghanistan she directed that a new cap badge be issued depicting the walls of the besieged town with the word 'Jellalabad' superscribed on the existing Light Infantry bugle horn.

It was all a far cry from the regiment's beginnings. It was raised in 1685 by Theophilus Hastings, 7th Earl of Huntingdon, who was one of the most prominent aristocratic supporters of the House of Stuart, having earlier been a bitter opponent. On the arrival of the Dutch fleet bringing William of Orange to England he marched his regiment down to Plymouth hoping to hold the citadel for James II. Instead, he was arrested, and although he was later freed rumours persisted that he was involved in Jacobite plots to return the Stuarts to the throne. Ironically, Huntingdon's regiment quickly transferred its loyalty to the House of Orange and it was involved in suppressing Jacobite rebellions in Scotland and Ireland, fighting at Killiecrankie in Scotland in 1689 and at the Boyne in Ireland the following year. As if that were not sufficient proof of the regiment's loyalty to the Crown, in 1746 it also fought in the Duke of Cumberland's army at the Battle of Culloden where it served under the title Pulteney's Regiment of Foot after Major General Harry Pulteney, Member of Parliament for Hedon in Yorkshire. The regimental history dryly noted that the day of the battle began with Prince Charles Edward Stuart being 'an imaginary monarch' and ended with him being 'a destitute fugitive'. Although the battle was a decisive victory for the British government and ended the Jacobite challenge once and for all, Culloden was never awarded as a battle honour to any of the regiments which took part in it.

The Somersets gave loyal service to thirteen monarchs; in addition to periods spent in India it also served in Europe, North America, the Caribbean, South Africa, Malaya and in both world wars. In 1959 the regiment amalgamated with The Duke of Cornwall's Light Infantry (32nd and 46th) to form The Somerset and Cornwall Light Infantry and in 1968 this became 1st Battalion of the newly formed Light Infantry. Later still, in 2007, its history and traditions were incorporated into The Rifles, a new large regiment representing the army's light infantry and rifle traditions. The Somerset's regimental museum is situated in the Somerset Military Museum, which is a part of the Museum of Somerset at Taunton Castle.

# Battle Honours

## Pre-1914

*Carried on the Regimental Colour*
**Gibraltar 1704–5, Dettingen, Martinique 1809, Ava, Ghuznee 1839, Afghanistan 1839, Cabool 1842, Sevastopol, South Africa 1878–9, Burmah 1885–87, Relief of Ladysmith, South Africa 1899–1902**

## First World War (18 battalions)

*Those in bold carried on the Queen's Colour*
Le Cateau, Retreat from Mons, Marne 1914, 18, Aisne 1914, Armentières 1914, **Ypres 1915, 17, 18**, St. Julien, Frezenberg, Bellewaarde, Hooge 1915, **Loos**, Mount Sorrel, **Somme 1916, 18, Albert 1916, 18**, Delville Wood, Guillemont, Flers-Courcelette, Morval, Le Transloy, Ancre 1916, 18, **Arras 1917, 18**, Vimy 1917, Scarpe 1917, 18, Arleux, Langemarck 1917, Menin Road, Polygon Wood, Broodseinde, Poelcappelle, Passchendaele, **Cambrai 1917, 18**, St. Quentin, Bapaume 1918, Rosières, Avre, Lys, Hazebrouck, Béthune, Soissonais-Ourq, Drocourt-Quéant, **Hindenburg Line**, Havrincourt, Épehy, Canal du Nord, Courtrai, Selle, Valenciennes, Sambre, France and Flanders 1914–18, Gaza, El Mughar, Nebi Samwil, Jerusalem, Megiddo, Sharon, **Palestine 1917, 18, Tigris 1916**, Sharqat, Mesopotamia 1916–18, N.W. Frontier India 1915

## Post-1918

*Carried on the Regimental Colour*
**Afghanistan 1919**

## Second World War

*Those in bold carried on the Queen's Colour*
Odon, Caen, **Hill 112, Mont Pincon,** Noireau Crossing, Seine 1944, Nederrijn, Geilenkirchen, Roer, **Rhineland,** Cleve, Goch, Hochwald, Xanten, **Rhine,** Bremen, **North-West Europe 1944–45, Cassino II,** Trasimene Line, Arezzo, Advance to Florence, Capture of Forli, **Cosina Canal Crossing, Italy 1944–45,** Athens, Greece 1944–45, **North Arakan,** Buthidaung, **Ngakyedauk Pass,** Burma 1943–44

## Recipients of the Victoria Cross

Sergeant William Napier, 13th Regiment, Indian Mutiny, 1857
Private Patrick Carlin, 13th Regiment, Indian Mutiny, 1858
Major (later Colonel) William Knox Leet, 13th Regiment, Zulu War, 1879
Private Thomas Henry Sage, 8th Battalion, First World War, 1917
Lieutenant George Albert Cairns, The Somerset Light Infantry, attached 1st South Staffordshire Regiment, Second World War, 1944

# The Lancashire Fusiliers

## 20th

Some acts of supreme courage take place in such extraordinary circumstances that they are unlikely ever to be
repeated. That was the case in the early morning of 25
April 1915 when six gallant men of 1st Battalion The
Lancashire Fusiliers were awarded the Victoria Cross
during the landings at W Beach on Cape Helles at the
beginning of the campaign against Turkish forces in
Gallipoli. Ever afterwards this exceptional event was
immortalised as 'the six VCs before breakfast' and later
the beach in question was renamed 'Lancashire Landing'.

During the first wave of the landings the 1st Battalion
was met by withering fire from hidden machine guns,
which caused a great number of casualties – eleven
officers and 350 men killed or wounded. The survivors,
however, rushed up the beach to cut barbed wire
entanglements and, despite continuing enemy fire, were
able to take the beach and the Turkish positions on the
cliffs above it. The recipients of the Victoria Cross were
elected by their fellow Fusiliers as having displayed the
greatest courage during their assault and their names
were gazetted in two citations, on 24 August 1915 and
13 March 1917: those of Captain Cuthbert Bromley,
Corporal John Grimshaw, Private William Keneally,

Sergeant Alfred Richards, Sergeant Frank Stubbs and Captain Richard Willis.

The regiment was also represented in the Gallipoli campaign by four Territorial battalions which served together in 125th Brigade and fought at the Second Battle of Krithia in May 1915. These were all from the regimental area: 1/5th Battalion from Bury, Radcliffe and Heywood; 1/6th Battalion from Rochdale, Middleton and Todmorden; 1/7th Battalion from Salford; and 1/8th Battalion, also from Salford. Altogether 1816 Lancashire Fusiliers died at Gallipoli and every year in April, on 'Gallipoli Sunday', a service of commemoration and remembrance is held in the Church of St Mary the Virgin in Bury, Lancashire, the regimental town.

To commemorate Bury's casualties of the First World War a memorial was unveiled outside Wellington Barracks in April 1922. Built of Portland stone it was designed by Sir Edwin Lutyens, who was also responsible for the Cenotaph in Whitehall in London and whose father and great-uncle had served in the regiment. In 2009 it was moved to the town centre outside the new regimental museum. The Wellington Barracks site on the Bolton Road was redeveloped at the same time and the only remaining building associated with the regiment is the Castle Armoury, which was built on the site of Bury Castle in 1868 as a drill hall for the use of the town's volunteers and later for the Territorial Army.

The other Lancashire town with a close regimental connection is Salford where four 'pals battalions' were raised in September 1914 as part of the drive to recruit men from the same localities or workplaces. These were 1st Salford Pals (15th Lancashire Fusiliers), 2nd Salford

The Staff of 3rd Battalion The Lancashire Fusiliers, first inspection in Malta in 1899. From left to right: Major Deane, Lieutenant and Adjutant Thone, Commanding Officer Major Flemming and Lieutenant and Quartermaster Mr Dunne.

Pals (16th Lancashire Fusiliers), 3rd Salford Pals (19th Lancashire Fusiliers) and 4th Salford Pals (20th Lancashire Fusiliers). Three of those battalions were in action together on the first day of the Somme, 1 July 1916, in the attack on Thiepval Ridge, and, of twenty-four officers and 650 men from the 1st Salford Pals who went into the attack, twenty-one officers and 449 men had become casualties by the end of the day, either killed, wounded or missing. Their sacrifice is commemorated on the Salford cenotaph, a memorial in Portland stone surmounted by the sphinx of the Lancashire Fusiliers with the word 'Egypt', which was unveiled in April 1922.

Among the more famous Lancashire Fusiliers who served in the regiment during the First World War was J.R.R. Tolkien, the future author of *The Lord of the Rings* and *The Hobbit*. Although born in South Africa, Tolkien had been brought up and educated in England, at King Edward's School in Birmingham and at Exeter College, Oxford. Unlike many of his contemporaries, Tolkien did not rush to enlist in the British Army immediately after the outbreak of war in August 1914. Instead he completed his studies at Oxford and was commissioned as a second lieutenant in 11th Lancashire Fusiliers in 1915. With them he saw action at the Battle of the Somme, acting as Signals Officer during the fighting at Ovillers-la-Boisselle where he witnessed what he called 'the animal horror of active service'.

Towards the end of the battle he contracted trench fever, a debilitating and potentially fatal condition transmitted by lice in the verminous trenches, and had to be invalided home. While convalescing he started writing 'The Book of Lost Tales', which eventually became *The*

*Silmarillion*, and it is likely that the imagery of the 'Dead Marshes' in *The Lord of the Rings* was inspired by his experiences on the Western Front. In spring 1918, while still in hospital, Tolkien received news that 11th Lancashire Fusiliers had been virtually wiped out during the fighting on the River Aisne. In the foreword to *The Lord of the Rings* he wrote: 'By 1918 all but one of my close friends were dead'. During the course of the war The Lancashire Fusiliers suffered some 13,000 casualties.

Curiously for a regiment so intimately connected to the county of Lancashire, it was raised in Exeter on 20 November 1688 by Sir Richard Peyton, a West Country landowner, for service in the forces loyal to the newly arrived Prince William of Orange. In 1751 it was numbered 20th (or XXth) Regiment of Foot and in 1782 received the territorial designation of East Devonshire and a second battalion was added in 1858. During this period the regiment was seldom out of the thick of the action. As Bligh's Regiment it served under the Duke of Cumberland at the Battle of Fontenoy in 1745 and a year later at the Battle of Culloden, which ended the Jacobite uprising.

During the subsequent Seven Years War, on 1 August 1759, the 20th was one of the six British infantry battalions (plus two Hanoverian) which defeated a superior French force of cavalry, a feat unparalleled in warfare at the time. The Battle of Minden occupies an honoured place in the history of the British Army. Not only did the attacking infantry regiments display steadiness and discipline while facing successive heavy cavalry charges but they triumphed in spite of being given the wrong orders. As a result, all six infantry regiments

Colour Party, 3rd Battalion The Lancashire Fusiliers, 1900. From left to right: Sergeant Inskip, 2nd Lieutenant Olive, Sergeant Richardson, 2nd Lieutenant Tanner, Sergeant Kingston.

received 'Minden' as a battle honour and every year Minden Day was commemorated with special parades when the officers and soldiers wore roses in their caps or bonnets. The custom was a reminder that their pre-decessors plucked wild roses and placed them in their hats as a means of identification before they went into the attack. In the course of the Peninsula campaign against the forces of Napoleonic France the 20th fought in all the major battles under the overall command of the Duke of Wellington. It also fought in the Crimean War and the 2nd Battalion was one of the British infantry battalions which fought at the disastrous Battle of Spion Kop during the Boer War.

Regimental Sergeant Major Barrett of The Lancashire Fusiliers, around 1922. His RSM's badge is on his lower left sleeve and amongst his medals is a Military Cross.

By 1873 the 20th had moved into Wellington Barracks in Bury which had been designated the 17th Infantry Brigade Depot as part of a national scheme to house infantry regiments in specific locations. As a result The 20th East Devonshire Regiment was renamed The Lancashire Fusiliers, becoming the county regiment of central Lancashire and embracing the four battalions of The Royal Lancashire Militia. At the end of the Boer War the regiment was awarded a primrose-yellow hackle as an honour for its service to the Crown. The Lancashire Fusiliers retained its individuality until 1968 when it amalgamated with England's other fusilier regiments – The Royal Northumberland Fusiliers, The Royal Warwickshire Fusiliers and The Royal Fusiliers (London Regiment) – to form the new Royal Regiment of Fusiliers, becoming its short-lived 4th Battalion, which was disbanded in 1970.

## Battle Honours

### Pre-1914

*Carried on the Regimental Colour*
Dettingen, Minden, Egmont-op-Zee, Egypt, Maida, Vimiera, Corunna, Vittoria, Pyrenees, Orthes, Toulouse, Peninsula, Alma, Inkerman, Sevastopol, Lucknow, Khartoum, Relief of Ladysmith, South Africa 1899–1902

### First World War (30 battalions)

*Those in bold carried on the Queen's Colour*
Le Cateau, **Retreat from Mons**, Marne 1914, **Aisne 1914, 18**, Armentières 1914, **Ypres 1915, 17, 18**, St. Julien, Bellewaarde,

Somme 1916, 18, Albert 1916, 18, Bazentin, Delville Wood,
Pozières, Ginchy, Flers-Courcelette, Morval, Thiepval,
Le Transloy, Ancre Heights, Ancre 1916, 18, **Arras 1917, 18,**
Scarpe 1917, 18, Arleux, Messines 1917, Pilckem,
Langemarck 1917, Menin Road, Polygon Wood, Broodseinde,
Poelcappelle, **Passchendaele, Cambrai 1917, 18,** St. Quentin,
Bapaume 1918, Rosières, Lys, Estaires, Hazebrouck, Bailleul,
Kemmel, Béthune, Scherpenberg, Amiens, Drocourt-Quéant,
**Hindenburg Line,** Épéhy, Canal du Nord, St. Quentin Canal,
Courtrai, Selle, Sambre, France and Flanders 1914–18,
Doiran 1917, **Macedonia 1915–18,** Helles, **Landing at Helles,**
Krithia, Suvla, Landing at Suvla, Scimitar Hill, Gallipoli 1915,
Rumani, Egypt 1915–17

## Second World War

*Those in bold carried on the Queen's Colour*
**Defence of Escaut,** St. Omer-La Bassée, **Caen,** North-West
Europe 1940, 44, **Medjez el Bab,** Oued Zarga, North Africa
1942–43, Adrano, Sicily 1943, Termoli, Trigno, **Sangro,**
**Cassino II,** Trasimene Line, Monte Ceco, Monte Spaduro,
Senio, **Argenta Gap,** Italy 1943–45, **Malta 1941–42,**
Rathedaung, Htizwe, **Kohima,** Naga Village, **Chindits 1944,**
**Burma 1943–45**

## Recipients of the Victoria Cross

Captain (Temporary Major) Cuthbert Bromley, 1st Battalion,
  First World War, 1915
Sergeant Frank Edward Stubbs, 1st Battalion, First World
  War, 1915
Lance-Corporal (later Lieutenant-Colonel) John Elisha
  Grimshaw, 1st Battalion, First World War, 1915
Captain (later Major) Richard Raymond Willis, 1st Battalion,
  First World War, 1915

Sergeant Alfred Joseph Richards, 1st Battalion, First World War, 1915

Private (later Lance Sergeant) William Stephen Keneally, 1st Battalion, First World War, 1915

Private John Lynn, 2nd Battalion, First World War, 1915

Private (later Corporal) James Hutchinson, 2/5th Battalion, First World War, 1916

Captain (Temporary Lieutenant Colonel) Bertram Best-Dunkley, 2/5th Battalion, First World War, 1917

Sergeant Joseph Lister, 1st Battalion, First World War, 1917

Second Lieutenant Bernard Matthew Cassidy, 2nd Battalion, First World War, 1918

Temporary Second Lieutenant John Schofield, 2/5th Battalion, First World War, 1918

Lance Corporal Joel Halliwell, 11th Battalion, First World War, 1918

Lance Sergeant (later Lieutenant) Edward Benn Smith, 1/5th Battalion, First World War

Acting Sergeant Harold John Colley, 10th Battalion, First World War, 1918

Private Frank Lester, 10th Battalion, First World War, 1918

Sergeant (later Regimental Sergeant Major) James Clarke, 15th Battalion, First World War, 1918

Acting Lieutenant Colonel James Neville Marshall, Irish Guards, Commanding 16th Battalion, First World War, 1918

Fusilier (later Lance Corporal) Francis Arthur Jefferson, 2nd Battalion, Second World War, 1944

# The South Wales Borderers

## 24th

One of the best known and most impressive scenes in the history of war films is the moment in Stanley Baker's hugely successful movie 1964 *Zulu* (which the Welsh actor produced and in which he also starred) when red-coated soldiers start to sing 'Men of Harlech' during their defence of Rorke's Drift. This notable incident followed the disastrous defeat of a British army under Lord Chelmsford at Isandlwana during the Zulu War of 1879 and in the eyes of the British public the brave stand went some way to restoring British military honour. As the men break into this well-known Welsh song of martial defiance, the meaning is clear: these are Welsh soldiers steadying their nerves as they face the overwhelming odds of the opposing Zulu army and hoping to match the battle chants of the massed impis. It is a great cinematic moment and it is rightly celebrated but the odds are that it never happened in the way it is portrayed in the film. According to Professor Saul David, the most recent historian of the battle, of the 113 infantrymen present at the mission station at Rorke's Drift in Natal on 22/23 January 1879, only twenty-seven had been born in Wales and of these sixteen were born in Monmouthshire, then an English county. Their senior NCO, Colour Sergeant

A group of men from 2nd Battalion The South Wales Borderers at Southampton prior to leaving England for the D-Day landing on 6 June 1944. They were the only unit of Welsh soldiers to land on D-Day.

Frank Bourne, was a Sussex man and Private Henry Hook, erroneously portrayed in the film as a drinker, came from Gloucestershire. They were all soldiers of B Company, 24th (2nd Warwickshire) Regiment which only became The South Wales Borderers two years later.

There were other historical inconsistencies but the fact remains that the film gave such a powerful portrayal of a small number of red-coated soldiers facing a heroic enemy that *Zulu* has become an icon of Welsh courage in battle. All told, the 2/24th won eleven Victoria Crosses that day, including two awarded posthumously to Lieutenant Nevil Coghill and Lieutenant Teignmouth Melvill for their gallant attempt to save the Colours during the Battle of Isandlwana. The Colours are now preserved in the Havard Chapel in Brecon Cathedral in recognition of the fact that, despite its original English territorial affiliation, the 24th Regiment had an existing connection with Wales. Before leaving for South Africa its depot had been established at Brecon to take advantage of the recruiting possibilities in the industrialised areas of the heads of the South Wales valleys. The barracks were built on the Watton in several stages during the nineteenth century and are still in use as the administrative headquarters of the army in Wales. Also on the site is the regimental museum which houses the Zulu Room commemorating the 24th's role at Rorke's Drift and Isandlwana.

Brecon is still a garrison town: located on its eastern edge is Dering Lines, a military complex that has been completely rebuilt in recent years and is very different from the hutted camp in which many Welsh soldiers trained during the two world wars of the last century. Now it forms part of the Infantry Battle School where the

Sergeant J. Roberts, 1st Battalion The South Wales Borderers, being presented with the Military Medal for 'Gallantry in defence of No. 11 Camp Picquet, Kach Camp Waziristan in May 1937'.

Colour Party 1st Battalion South Wales Borderers parading at Brecon Beacons Barracks on 1 April 1934 prior to the laying up of the Colours in Brecon Cathedral.

Seven Victoria Cross holders of the South Wales Borderers at Brecon in 1898 for the unveiling of the Zulu War memorial: Private Robert Jones VC, Private A. H. Hook VC, Private William Jones VC, Private David Bell VC, Colonel E. S. Browne VC, Private Frederick Hitch VC, Private John Williams VC.

British Army trains its junior officers and non-commissioned officers in battlefield tactics. Just a few miles further west is the Sennybridge Army Camp and Training Area, one of the largest ranges and training centres in the UK. Many thousands of service personnel use these facilities each year, training on the rugged Brecon Beacons; among them are candidates for the elite Special Air Service regiment (SAS).

The South Wales Borderers was raised in 1689 as Dering's Regiment of Foot, its founder being a supporter of the House of Orange, Sir Edward Dering of Surrenden, near Pluckley in Kent. It saw action in most of the campaigns fought by the British Army in the eighteenth century but had the misfortune to be part of General Sir John Burgoyne's army that surrendered to American forces at Saratoga in 1777. By then it had become the 24th Foot and in 1782 it was given a territorial association with Warwickshire, although for some time its depot was in Manchester. One of the most unusual awards of the Victoria Cross occurred when the 24th was based in Burma and a party of seventeen men was sent to the Andaman Islands in May 1867 to investigate the disappearance of an earlier group, thought to have been killed by cannibals. They, too, were attacked by natives on landing and five men were put ashore from the steamer *Assam Valley* to rescue them during a raging storm. All were saved and the men involved – Privates David Bell, James Cooper, William Griffiths, Thomas Murphy and Assistant-Surgeon Campbell Mellis – were awarded the VC for extraordinary courage in the face of great danger.

Following the reforms of 1881 the 24th was renamed The South Wales Borderers, becoming the county regiment of Brecknockshire, Cardiganshire, Monmouthshire, Montgomeryshire and Radnorshire with two Regular battalions and two Militia battalions – 3rd Battalion, formerly the Royal South Wales Borderers Militia (Royal Radnor and Brecknock Rifles) and 4th Battalion, formerly the Royal Montgomery and Merioneth Rifles Militia. During the First World War the regiment raised nineteen Territorial or Service battalions composed largely of men from its home recruiting counties in South Wales.

Among them was a group of leading Welsh rugby union players. The best known was Charlie Pritchard of Newport who won thirteen caps and was a member of

Members of 1st Battalion The South Wales Borderers who went to France in August 1914 and came home with the Battalion in 1919: Sergeant A. E. Ravenhill MM, CSM G. Saunders MM, Sergeant G. Gibbs MM with bar, Captain C. A. Baker MC, RSM J. Shirley MC.

Amalgamation parade of The South Wales Borderers and The Welsh Regiment to form The Royal Regiment of Wales at Cardiff Castle in June 1969.

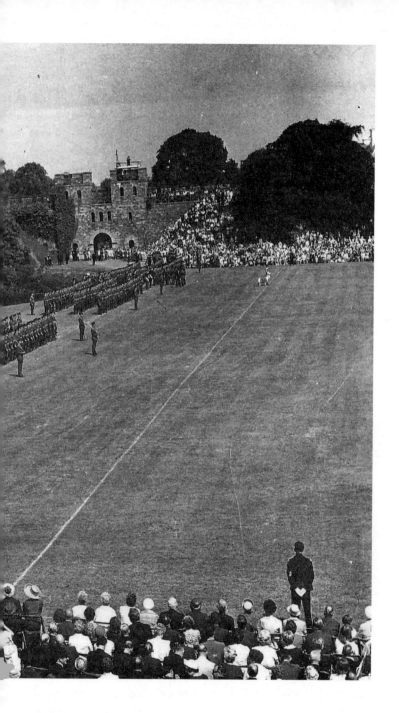

the Welsh XV that beat the New Zealand All Blacks in 1905. He was killed in action during the Battle of the Somme in 1916 while serving with 12th South Wales Borderers. The other wartime international players were Jack Jenkins from Caerphilly, who had been capped by Wales against South Africa in 1906, David Phillips Jones of Pontypool, who scored a try in his only game against Ireland in 1907, and Walter Martin of Newport, who was capped twice in 1912, against Ireland and France. Another notable Welshman in the regiment was the poet and dramatist Saunders Lewis who went on to become one of the founders of the Welsh Nationalist Party (Plaid Cymru) in 1925.

In the period between the two world wars the 1st Battalion served in Hong Kong and India while the 2nd Battalion also saw service in India and in 1936 was involved in quelling the Arab Revolt in Palestine. At the outbreak of war in 1939 the 1st Battalion was still in India and two years later took part in the Allied operation to oust the government in Iraq to prevent the country's oil supplies falling into German hands. In the following year it served in North Africa and sustained horrific casualties: during an attempted breakout from Tobruk only four officers and a hundred men survived and the battalion ceased to exist. To the 2nd Battalion fell the honour of being the only Welsh formation to take part in the D-Day landings in June 1944 and it ended its war in Hamburg. Another battalion – 6th South Wales Borderers – fought in Burma as part of the Fourteenth 'Forgotten' Army. It began its war as a Territorial battalion based at Glanusk Park near Crickhowell and was originally retrained in armoured warfare before reverting to infantry for service in Burma. One of its officers was Alun Lewis, the poet and short story writer from Cwmaman, near Aberdare in Glamorganshire. A pacifist before the war, he joined up in the Royal Engineers in 1940 before being commissioned in 6th South Wales Borderers. If the war hastened Lewis's development as a writer – during that period he produced four volumes containing twenty-five stories and ninety-five poems, including the well-known elegy 'All Day It Has Rained' – it also hastened his death. Lewis died in an unexplained accident with a revolver while visiting a forward position near Chittagong on 5 March 1944.

After the war the 2nd Battalion was disbanded and on 11 June 1969 1st South Wales Borderers amalgamated with 1st Welch Regiment to form The Royal Regiment of Wales with its headquarters at Maindy Barracks in Cardiff. A further change came in 2006 when the regiment amalgamated with The Royal Welch Fusiliers to form the 2nd Battalion of The Royal Welsh Regiment. Four years later the new regiment was reduced in size when the 2nd Battalion was ordered to merge with the 1st Battalion, taking with it the history and traditions of The South Wales Borderers.

---

## Battle Honours

### Pre-1914

*Carried on the Regimental Colour*
**Blenheim, Ramilles, Oudenarde, Malplaquet, Egypt, Cape of Good Hope 1806, Talavera, Busaco, Fuentes d'Onoro,**

Salamanca, Vittoria, Pyrenees, Nivelle, Orthes, Peninsular, Chillianwala, Goojerat, Punjaub, South Africa 1877–89, Burma 1885–87, South Africa 1900–02

## First World War (19 battalions)

*Those in bold carried on the Queen's Colour*
**Mons,** Retreat from Mons, **Marne 1914,** Aisne 1914, 18, **Ypres 1914, 17, 18,** Langemarck 1914,17, **Gheluvelt,** Nonne Bosschen, Givenchy 1914, Aubers, Loos, **Somme 1916, 18,** Bazentin, Pozières, Flers-Courcelette, Morval, Ancre Heights, Ancre 1916, Arras 1917, 18, Scarpe 1917, Messines 1917, 18, Pilckem, Menin Road, Polygon Wood, Broodseinde, Poelcappelle, Passchendaele, **Cambrai 1917, 18,** St. Quentin, Bapaume 1918, Lys, Estaires, Hazebrouck, Bailleul, Kemmel, Béthune, Scherpenberg, Drocourt-Quéant, Hindenburg Line, Havrincourt, Épéhy, St. Quentin Canal, Beaurevoir, Courtrai, Selle, Valenciennes, Sambre, France and Flanders 1914–18, **Doiran 1917, 18,** Macedonia 1915–18, Helles, **Landing at Helles,** Krithia, Suvla, Sari Bair, Scimitar Hill, Gallipoli 1915–16, Egypt 1916, Tigris 1916, Kut el Amara 1917, **Baghdad,** Mesopotamia 1916–18, **Tsingtao**

## Second World War

*Those in bold carried on the Queen's Colour*
**Norway 1940, Normandy Landing, Sully, Caen,** Falaise, Risle Crossing, **Le Havre,** Antwerp-Turnhout Canal, Scheldt, Zetten, Arnhem 1945, **North-West Europe 1944–45,** Gazala, **North Africa 1942,** North Arakan, **Mayu Tunnels, Pinwe,** Shweli, Myitson, **Burma 1944–45**

## Recipients of the Victoria Cross

Private (later Sergeant) David Bell, 2nd Battalion,
  24th Regiment of Foot, Andaman Islands, 1867

Private James Cooper, 2nd Battalion, 24th Regiment of Foot,
  Andaman Islands, 1867

Assistant Surgeon (later Lieutenant Colonel) Campbell Mellis
  Douglas, 2nd Battalion, 24th Regiment of Foot, Andaman
  Islands, 1867

Private William Griffiths, 2nd Battalion, 24th Regiment of
  Foot, Andaman Islands, 1867

Private Thomas Murphy, 2nd Battalion, 24th Regiment of
  Foot, Andaman Islands, 1867

Lieutenant Edric Frederick Gifford, The Lord Gifford,
  2nd Battalion, 24th Regiment of Foot, First Ashanti
  Expedition, 1874

Corporal (later Sergeant) William Wilson Allen, 2nd Battalion,
  24th Regiment of Foot, Zulu War, 1879

Lieutenant (later Major) Gonville Bromhead, 2nd Battalion,
  24th Regiment of Foot, Zulu War, 1879

Lieutenant (later Brigadier) Edward Stevenson Browne,
  1st Battalion, 24th Regiment of Foot, Zulu War, 1879

Lieutenant Nevill Josiah Aylmer Coghill, 1st Battalion,
  24th Regiment of Foot, Zulu War, 1879

Private Frederick Hitch, 2nd Battalion, 24th Regiment of
  Foot, Zulu War, 1879

Private (later Sergeant) Alfred Henry Hook, 2nd Battalion,
  24th Regiment of Foot, Zulu War, 1879

Private Robert Jones, 2nd Battalion, 24th Regiment of Foot,
  Zulu War, 1879

Private William Jones, 2nd Battalion, 24th Regiment of Foot,
  Zulu War, 1879

Lieutenant Teignmouth Melvill, 1st Battalion, 24th Regiment
  of Foot, Zulu War, 1879

Private (later Sergeant) John Williams, 2nd Battalion,
24th Regiment of Foot, Zulu War, 1879

Temporary Captain Angus Buchanan, 4th Battalion,
First World War, 1916

Private James Henry Fynn, 4th Battalion, First World
War, 1916

Company Sergeant Major Ivor Rees, 11th Battalion, First
World War, 1917

Sergeant Albert White, 2nd Battalion, First World War, 1917

Temporary Lieutenant Colonel Daniel Burges, The
Gloucestershire Regiment, Commanding 7th South Wales
Borderers, First World War, 1918

Acting Lieutenant Colonel Dudley Graham Johnson, The
South Wales Borderers, attached 2nd Royal Sussex
Regiment, 1918

Company Sergeant Major John (Jack) Henry Williams, 10th
Battalion, First World War, 1918

# The Cameronians (Scottish Rifles)

## 26th and 90th

On a pleasant early summer's day, 14 May 1968, The Cameronians (Scottish Rifles) disbanded and marched into history rather than amalgamate with another Scottish regiment. Surrounded by the green rolling hills of the Scottish Lowlands, this famous fighting regiment paraded on the same spot where it had been formed exactly 279 years earlier near Douglas in Lanarkshire, the regiment's spiritual heartland. Towering above the men as they marched in at the traditional 140 paces per minute of a rifle regiment was the statue of their founder, the Earl of Douglas. It was a sad and sonorous occasion yet the padre, the Revd Dr David McDonald, told the men on parade to be of good cheer: 'Today, you cease to be a regular arm of Her Majesty's forces. It has never been the habit of Cameronians to whimper and we shall not whimper now, for, thank God, we can fill this doleful moment with gratitude and pride.'

The Cameronians had the unique distinction within the British Army of being named after a religious sect whose aim was to maintain Presbyterian worship in Scotland following the accession to the British throne of William and Mary of Orange. As such, the regiment was raised to defend the rights of the Convention of Estates

Men of The Cameronians (Scottish Rifles) gather around a universal carrier to listen to Piper A. Mackay on 4 October 1943.

(the Scottish government) and to pledge loyalty to the new joint monarchy, but it took its name from the followers of Richard Cameron, a militant Protestant who had renounced allegiance to the House of Stuart. Later, in 1751, the regiment was numbered the 26th Foot but it was always referred to by its original name.

The regiment also embraced another distinctive British military tradition, that of the light infantry; this came about in 1881 as a result of the Cardwell/Childers reforms when the 26th amalgamated with the 90th Perthshire Light Infantry. The new regiment was composed of two battalions and while it was known as The Cameronians, the 2nd Battalion was always referred to as The Scottish Rifles. Relations between these two very different regimental forbears were not always cordial and did not improve until after the First World War.

Both regiments had seen extensive service in Europe during the eighteenth and nineteenth centuries. The 26th fought under the Duke of Marlborough during the War of the Spanish Succession and was in action at the great victories at Blenheim, Ramillies, Oudenarde and Malplaquet. At the end of the campaign one of the officers, Captain John Blackader, was moved to record his low opinion of the enemy: 'I observe this of the French that they are the most easily beat and cowed of any people in the world, did we but second Providence in pushing them when the opportunity is put in our hand.'

The 90th Perthshire Light Infantry had an equally illustrious history. Its founder was Thomas Graham of Balgowan, later Lord Lynedoch, whose wife, Mary Cathcart, was one of the great beauties of her day, her portrait being painted four times by Thomas

Gainsborough. Her death from consumption in 1792 prompted her husband to join the army as a private soldier and then to raise his new regiment, whose first major action was at the Battle of Aboukir Bay in 1800 to expel French forces under the command of Napoleon Bonaparte. After serving in Ceylon (Sri Lanka) and South Africa, the 90th Perthshire Light Infantry was sent to the Crimea in 1854 and played a role in the siege of the Russian fortress of Sevastopol. The regimental medical officer, Dr Douglas Arthur Reid, left a graphic account of the appalling conditions facing the men during that first winter of the war and which led to a public outcry at home:

> When I awoke in the morning my bed was covered with snow and ice and the floor of my tent was deep in snow. It was dreadful in the trenches at this time, and the men suffered terribly. For twenty-four hours at a stretch they were unable to lie down, the trenches being full of snow or water.

During the war, which ended in 1856, the regiment suffered more than 200 casualties, most of them lost to disease and the cold.

Following the amalgamation, The 2nd Scottish Rifles served in the Boer War of 1899–1902 and both battalions were sent to France in August 1914 on the outbreak of war with Germany. In addition the regiment raised nine service battalions for war service as well as four battalions of the Territorial Force. The latter were part-time soldiers drawn from a variety of backgrounds. When John Reith, later the founding father of the BBC, was commissioned in 1/5th Scottish Rifles in 1911 he observed that the 'social class of the man in the ranks was higher than that of any other regiment in Glasgow'.

Whole companies were formed from the staff of Glasgow's leading business firms and one was raised from the University of Glasgow with the result that many of the rank and file were educated members of the middle class who thought themselves equal to, if not better than, any regular regiment. Among those who served in The Cameronians were two future prime ministers, Arthur Bonar Law and Sir Henry Campbell-Bannerman, and the scientist William Thomson, later Lord Kelvin. By way of contrast, the 1/6th Battalion drew its men from the heavy industrial towns of Lanarkshire and the 1/7th Battalion had one company of total abstainers while the 1/8th Battalion drew one of its companies from Glasgow's breweries.

During the fighting The Cameronians suffered 7,106 casualties killed and 11,000 wounded while four soldiers were awarded the Victoria Cross. Their sacrifice is marked by an arresting war memorial in Glasgow's Kelvingrove Park showing an attacking soldier, rifle in hand, alongside a machine-gunner and a fallen comrade. It was a similar story in the Second World War when the regiment provided two Regular battalions and three Territorial battalions for the fighting in France, Italy, the Middle East and Burma. The 1st Battalion served with the Chindits in Burma. It was renowned for its toughness and one Chindit officer, the novelist and historian John Masters, quickly recognised the qualities Cameronians brought to the force: 'No one but their own officers could handle them, and their touchy discipline vanished

Sergeant Major Kirk stands with a sergeant and a corporal at the gates of Winston Barracks in Lanark, depot of The Cameronians (Scottish Rifles). The date is 13 August 1955.

altogether for a week around the great Scottish fiesta of Hogmanay, New Year's Eve.'

In the post-war period The Cameronians were deployed in counter-terrorism duties in Malaya and Aden but their days were numbered. In a decision that was controversial at the time and still causes comment, The Cameronians chose disbandment when defence cutbacks were announced in 1967. For a regiment steeped in the covenanting tradition it was fitting that the final parade culminated in a conventicle, an outdoor service, with the communion table standing on a spur of ground close to Castle Dangerous, the former Douglas stronghold. Piquets were then posted to protect the conventicle, a necessary precaution in the covenanting days and a custom preserved by The Cameronians. The regiment also maintained the tradition of presenting a copy of the Holy Bible to each new recruit.

During its lifetime The Cameronians provided the British Army with an impressive number of distinguished soldiers including three field marshals – Viscount Hill, who served under Wellington in the Peninsula and at Waterloo; Viscount Wolseley, one of the great Victorian army reformers; and Sir Evelyn Wood, a holder of the Victoria Cross. Always tough and enduring in battle, The Cameronians reflected the character of its main recruitment area – the industrial areas of Glasgow and Lanarkshire – and in later years took quiet pride when the Germans nicknamed its stocky and aggressive soldiers *Giftzwerge*, or poison dwarfs.

In the early days Cameronian soldiers wore the red tunic and white breeches of a line infantry regiment of the British Army but in 1891 they were authorised to wear trews of Douglas tartan in recognition of the regiment's links to the family.

# Battle Honours

## Pre-1914

*Carried on the Regimental Colour*
**Blenheim, Ramilies, Oudenarde, Malplaquet, Mandora, Corunna, Martinique 1809, Guadaloupe 1810, South Africa 1846–47, Sevastopol, Lucknow, Abyssinia, South Africa 1979, 78, 79 Relief of Ladysmith, South Africa 1899–1902**

## The First World War (27 battalions)

*Those in bold carried on the Queen's Colour*
**Mons,** Le Cateau, Retreat from Mons, **Marne 1914–18,** Aisne 1914, La Basseé 1914, Armentiéres 1914, **Neuve Chapelle,** Aubers, **Loos, Somme 1916–18,** Albert 1916, Bazentin, Pozières, Flers-Courcelette, Scherpenberg, Le Transloy, Ancre Heights, Arras 1917–18, Scarpe 1917–18, Arleux, **Ypres 1917, 18,** Pilckem, Langemarck 1917, Menin Road, Polygon Wood, Passchendaele, St Quentin, Rosières, Avre, Lys, Hazebrouck, Bailleul, Kemmel, Scherpenberg, Soissonnais-Ourcq, Drocourt-Quéant, **Hindenburg Line,** Epéhy, Canal du Nord, St Quentin Canal, Cambrai 1918, Courtrai, Selle, Sambre, France and Flanders 1914–18, Doiran 1917, 18, **Macedonia 1915–18, Gallipoli 1915–16,** Rumani, Egypt 1916–17, Gaza, El Mughar, Nebi Shamwil, Jaffa, **Palestine 1917–18**

## The Second World War

*Those in bold carried on the Queen's Colour*
Ypres-Commines Canal, **Odon,** Cheux, Caen, Mont Pincon, Estry, Nederrijn, **Scheldt,** South Beveland, Walcheren Causeway, Asten, Roer, **Rhineland,** Reichswald, Moyland, **Rhine,** Dreierwalde, Bremen, Artlenberg, **North-West Europe 1940, 44–45,** Landing in Sicily, Simeto Bridgehead, Garigliano

Crossing, **Anzio,** Advance to Tiber, **Italy 1943–44,** Pogu 1942, Paungde, Yenangyaung 1942, **Chindits 1944, Burma 1942, 44**

## Recipients of the Victoria Cross

Private John Alexander, 90th Perthshire Light Infantry, Crimea, 1855

Sergeant (later Captain) Andrew Moynihan, 90th Perthshire Light Infantry, Crimea, 1855

Surgeon Anthony Home, 90th Perthshire Light Infantry, Indian Mutiny, 1857

Assistant-Surgeon William Bradshaw, 90th Perthshire Light Infantry, Indian Mutiny, 1857

Major (later Lieutenant General) John Guise, 90th Perthshire Light Infantry, Indian Mutiny, 1857

Sergeant Samuel Hill, 90th Perthshire Light Infantry, Indian Mutiny, 1857

Private Patrick Graham, 90th Perthshire Light Infantry, Indian Mutiny, 1857

Lieutenant William Rennie, 90th Perthshire Light Infantry, Indian Mutiny, 1857

Lieutenant (later Lieutenant Colonel) William Lysons, 90th Perthshire Light Infantry, Zulu War, 1879

Private (later Colour Sergeant) Edmund Fowler, 90th Perthshire Light Infantry, Zulu War, 1879

Private (later Lieutenant) Henry May, 1st Battalion, First World War, 1914

Lance Corporal (later Sergeant) John MacLaren Erskine, 5th Battalion, First World War, 1916

Private James Towers, 2nd Battalion, First World War, 1918

# The Royal Inniskilling Fusiliers

## 27th and 108th

Enniskillen, the most westerly town in the British Isles, is the only place in the United Kingdom to have given its name (in an alternative spelling) to two regiments – The Royal Inniskilling Dragoon Guards, a cavalry regiment, and The Royal Inniskilling Fusiliers, a line infantry regiment. Although both regiments lost their titles through amalgamation with other regiments in the latter part of the twentieth century their connection to the town is still commemorated in the historic castle of Enniskillen, on the banks of the River Erne in County Fermanagh. The infantry regiment was raised in Enniskillen in June 1689 by Colonel Zachariah Tiffin to counter the threat posed by forces loyal to King James II, who was attempting to regain his throne from William of Orange by fomenting an uprising in Ireland. The men of Enniskillen took part in the defeat of the Jacobites (as James's supporters were known) at nearby Newtownbutler and were present at the decisive Battle of the Boyne fought on 1 July 1690, which brought the rebellion to an end.

As was the case with all regiments of this period the regiment took its name from its Colonel and in 1745–46, as Blakeney's Regiment, it took part in the operations against the rebel Jacobite army commanded by Prince

Charles Edward Stuart. William Blakeney was one of the most experienced commanders in the Duke of Cumberland's army – he was described as a 'tough, scarred Irishman' – and during the Battle of Culloden Blakeney's Regiment served in the third line of the government army. It also took part in the pacification of the western Highlands after the battle. In 1751 it was numbered the 27th Foot and in 1782 received the territorial designation Enniskillen, with the spelling being changed to the alternative Inniskilling in 1840. The Gaelic form of the town's name is *Inis Ceithleann* (Kathleen's island), which lends itself to several English translations, but whatever the version the regiment was always nicknamed 'The Skins', as were the Dragoon Guards.

The regiment's greatest moment in history came during the Battle of Waterloo on 18 June 1815 when they saved the right wing of Wellington's army following a ferocious French cavalry attack at a point on the Allied line behind La Haye Sainte. Of the 15 officers present 14 were killed and 498 of the 670 other ranks were either killed or wounded during the fighting (the numbers vary). All the dead were found still lying in the form of their defensive square, not having yielded an inch of ground to their assailants. When the 40th Foot, one of the other regiments in the line, offered to lend the 27th some officers to replace the casualties the surviving officer, Major John Hare, refused, saying 'the sergeants liked to command the companies, and I would be loath to deprive them of such honour'. Ever afterwards Waterloo Day was celebrated each year on the anniversary with a parade commanded by the regiment's senior non-commissioned officers. In the aftermath of the fighting Napoleon was heard to offer

General Georges of the French Army, accompanied by Lord Gort, Commander-in-Chief of the British Expeditionary Force, inspecting 2nd Battalion The Royal Inniskilling Fusiliers at Bethune on 23 April 1940.

the following tribute: 'I have seen Russian, Prussian and French bravery, but anything to equal the stubborn bravery of the Regiment with castles in their caps I never before witnessed.' The reference was to the walled castle of Enniskillen on the regiment's Fusilier cap badge.

That connection to the town and its castle notwithstanding, when the 27th amalgamated with the 108th Regiment of Foot (Madras Infantry) in 1881 to form The Royal Inniskilling Fusiliers, the new regiment's depot was situated at St Lucia Barracks in the town of Omagh, County Tyrone. The handsome walled Victorian structure is still in existence and awaiting a new non-military role. As for the 108th Regiment, which became the Skins' 2nd Battalion, it started life in 1854 in the service of the Honourable East India Company as the 3rd Madras (European) Regiment and formally became part of the British Army in 1862. On amalgamation the new regiment's Militia and Volunteer battalions were 3rd Battalion (Fermanagh Light Infantry), 4th Battalion (Royal Tyrone Fusiliers) and 5th Battalion (The Prince of Wales's Own Donegal Militia). Until 1922 and the creation of the Irish Free State, which removed County Donegal from the regimental area, the Inniskillings recruited from Counties Fermanagh, Londonderry and Tyrone.

At the outbreak of the First World War the 1st Battalion was based in India and did not return to England until the beginning of 1915 when it came under the command of 29th Division and moved to Rugby. That sealed its fate as the division was soon earmarked for service in Gallipoli, which was also the destination of the 5th and 6th Battalions, both raised as volunteer battalions in Omagh on the outbreak of war. They took part in the landings at

Suvla Bay in August 1915 where casualties were heavy among the landing force largely due to Allied indecision and bloody-minded Turkish defence. As the 5th Inniskillings attempted to make some headway on the Kiretch Tepe position they found that their way forward was hampered by primitive Turkish landmines. This came as a rude shock to one young subaltern, 2nd Lieutenant Ivone Kirkpatrick: 'I felt strangely exalted and told my sergeant that I was enjoying myself. Not long after someone trod on a land mine a few yards away. I felt less exalted and rather frightened.' Later in his career, Kirkpatrick served in the Foreign Office as the Permanent Under-Secretary, Britain's senior diplomat.

Being based in Dover, the 2nd Battalion crossed over to France on 22 August and was soon in action in the initial fighting against the Germans. It would soon be joined by the 7th, 8th, 9th (Tyrone), 10th (Derry) and 11th (Donegal and Fermanagh) battalions, also made up of volunteers from the regimental recruiting area. The latter three battalions served in the 36th (Ulster) Division which went into the attack in the opening minutes of the first day of the Somme on 1 July 1916 and quickly encountered heavy enemy machine-gun fire. 'The losses of that day made mourning in many Ulster homes,' wrote their historian, Sir Frank Fox, who served on Haig's staff, 'but with the mourning there was pride that the Province had once again proved the steadfastness of its loyal courage'. Some 5,500 Ulstermen were killed in the assault on the Schwaben Redoubt and their names are remembered on Ulster Tower, which marks the extreme northern edge of the Ulstermen's advance. Dominating the area is a replica of Helen's Tower at Clandeboye, near Belfast.

Men of 11th Battalion The Royal Inniskilling Fusiliers in a captured German communications trench near Havrincourt during the Battle of Cambrai, November 1917.

The Inniskillings were also known as a literary regiment. Among their officers in the First World War was the distinguished poet and dramatist Edward Plunkett, Lord Dunsany, one of the leading Irish writers of his day and a man of considerable influence. Through his patronage he offered encouragement to the nationalist poet Francis Ledwidge who joined the 5th Battalion in October 1914 and was killed three years later during the Battle of Passchendaele. It is also probable that the 'Willie McBride' of Eric Bogle's famous anti-war song 'The Green Fields of France' served in the Inniskillings. Willie was the son of Joseph and Lena McBride, of Roan Cottage, Lislea, Armagh, and attended Crosskeys National School. He is buried at Authuile Military Cemetery, near Albert and Beaumont-Hamel, and his grave marker (Grave A. 36) inspired Bogle's famous opening lines:

> Well, how do you do, Private William McBride,
> Do you mind if I sit down here by your graveside?

Given the role played by the regiment in the battle it was entirely fitting that the anniversary of the first day of the Somme should have been chosen as the date in 1968 when the Inniskillings lost their separate identity when they amalgamated with The Royal Ulster Rifles and The Royal Irish Fusiliers to form The Royal Irish Rangers. After amalgamation with the Ulster Defence Regiment it became part of The Royal Irish Regiment which emerged in its latest form in 2007 with its headquarters at Palace Barracks, Holywood, Belfast.

# Battle Honours

## Pre-1914

*Carried on the Regimental Colour*
**Martinique 1762, Havannah, St Lucia 1778–96, Maida,
Busaco, Badajoz, Salamanca, Vittoria, Pyrenees, Nivelle,
Orthes, Toulouse, Peninsula, Waterloo, South Africa 1835,
1846–47, Central India, Relief of Ladysmith, South Africa
1899–1902**

## First World War (13 battalions)

*Those in bold carried on the Queen's Colour*
**Le Cateau,** Retreat from Mons, Marne 1914, Aisne 1914,
Messines 1914–17, Armentieres 1914, Aubers, Festubert
1915, **Somme 1916, 18,** Albert 1916, Bazentin, Guillemont,
Ginchy, Ancre 1916, Arras 1917, Scarpe 1917, **Ypres 1917, 18,**
Pilckem, Langemarck 1917, Polygon Wood, Broodseinde,
Poel Cappelle, Cambrai 1917–18, **St Quentin,** Rosieres,
**Hindenburg Line,** Beaurevoir, Courtrai, Selle, Sambre, **France
and Flanders 1915–18,** Kosturino, Struma, **Macedonia
1915–18,** Helles, Krithia, Suvla, Landing at Suvla, Scimitar
Hill, **Gallipoli 1915–16,** Egypt 1916, Gaza, Jerusalem,
Tel Azur, **Palestine 1917–18**

## Second World War

*Those in bold carried on the Queen's Colour*
Defence of Arras, Ypres-Comines Canal, **North-West Europe
1940,** Two Tree Hill, Bou Arada, Oued Zarga, Djebel El
Mahdi, **Djebel Tanngoucha, North Africa 1942–43,** Landing
in Sicily, Solarino, Simeto Bridgehead, Adrano, Simeto
Crossing, Pursuit to Messina, **Sicily 1943,** Termoli, Trigno, San
Salvo, Sangro, **Garigliano Crossing,** Minturno, Anzio, **Cassino
II,** Massa Tambourini, Liri Valley, Rome, Advance to the Tiber,

Trasimene Line, Monte Spaduro, Argenta Gap, **Italy 1943–45**, Middle East 1942, **Yenangyaung 1942**, Donbaik, **Burma 1942–43**

## Recipients of the Victoria Cross

Captain Gerald Robert O'Sullivan, 1st Battalion, First World War, 1915

Sergeant James Somers, 1st Battalion, First World War, 1915.

Captain Eric Norman Frankland Bell, The Royal Inniskilling Fusiliers, attached 4th Trench Mortar Battery, First World War, 1916

Lieutenant Colonel John Sherwood-Kelly CMG, The Norfolk Regiment, Commanding 1st Battalion, First World War, 1917

2nd Lieutenant James Samuel Emerson, 9th Battalion, First World War, 1917

Private James Duffy, 6th Battalion, First World War, 1917

Lance Corporal Ernest Seaman, 2nd Battalion, First World War, 1918

Private Norman Harvey, 1st Battalion, First World War, 1918

# The Gloucestershire Regiment

## 28th and 61st

To The Gloucestershire Regiment belongs the unique honour of being the only British line infantry regiment to be awarded the US Presidential Unit Citation, presented to units of the armed forces of the United States of America and its allies for extraordinary heroism in action against an armed enemy. The 'Glorious Glosters' were honoured in this way following their gallant last stand at the Battle of the Imjin River on 25 April 1951 during the Korean War. Many of the men were conscripts or reservists but, as was noted at the time, they lived up to the precepts of a proud history and the effect was felt throughout the whole of the British Army. According to the official communiqué 'the Chinese attacked on every side, screaming, blowing bugles, ringing bells and clashing cymbals. But the Gloucesters held them and fought back, not giving an inch of ground.' Of those men of Gloucestershire who tried to break out and reach the safety of 29 Brigade's lines, only 5 officers and 41 men made it, while 19 officers and 505 men went into Chinese captivity and two years of hardship and deprivation; of those 34 died.

But the stand made by the Gloucesters on the Imjin had not been in vain. The impetus of the Chinese advance

The return of the 'Glorious Glosters'. At Southampton docks a
tender brings ashore 150 British prisoners of war recently released
from Korean captivity. Amongst them is Lieutenant Colonel
J. P. Carne, VC. Standing on the right is Mrs A. E. Colburn,
of Lambourne, waiting on the quayside with her children.

had been halted and the brief respite allowed US reinforcements to be rushed into the defensive area to steady the line. For his gallant behaviour during and after the battle the commanding officer, Lieutenant Colonel James Carne, was awarded the Victoria Cross. On the battalion's return home in 1953 the survivors paraded through Gloucester before taking part in a service of thanksgiving in the cathedral where a memorial window to the Gloucesters' role in the Korean War was unveiled in 1997. Also on display in the cathedral is the Carne Cross, a 25cm high stone Celtic cross which Carne carved, using a nail, while in solitary confinement. In 2010 it was chosen to represent Gloucestershire as part of the BBC's *A History of the World* project with the British Museum.

The action in Korea was not the first time the Gloucesters had faced such overwhelming odds. During the Battle of Alexandria, fought in Egypt on 21 March 1801, the 28th (North Gloucestershire) Regiment bore the brunt of the initial French assault when they were simultaneously attacked by French cavalry from the rear. To meet this fresh challenge the rear ranks simply turned around to face the enemy and both attacks were repelled. To commemorate this unique feat the regiment was permitted to wear a small replica regimental badge on the back of their headdress, a fitting tribute to a regiment which enjoyed the nickname of 'The Slashers' – a reference to an unfortunate incident in Canada in 1764 when a Montreal merchant fell foul of some Gloucestershire soldiers and had part of his right ear cut off during the subsequent melee.

Formed in Portsmouth in 1694 by Colonel John Gibson, the original regiment became the 28th Foot in

1751 and was given the territorial designation North Gloucestershire in 1782. During the Napoleonic Wars the regiment served in the Peninsula campaign as well as in the last hundred days which culminated in the battles of Quatre Bras and Waterloo. The former battle was commemorated in 1875 in a famous painting by Elizabeth Thompson, Lady Butler: it shows the 28th in action, having formed a square in a field of rye and 'bracing itself for one massive, final charge of terrifying Polish Lancers and cuirassier veterans led by Marshal Ney'. The regiment also fought in the Crimean War and saw action at the battles of the Alma, Inkerman and Sevastopol. For much of that conflict the regiment was under the command of Lieutenant Colonel Henry Bentinck of the Coldstream Guards, who was later a general and a Groom-in-Waiting to Queen Victoria.

The second component of the regiment was no less distinguished. The 61st Foot was raised in 1756 as the 2nd Battalion of the 3rd Regiment of Foot (The Buffs) and was given the designation South Gloucestershire in 1782. Its first Colonel was Major General Granville Elliott, who had served with distinction in Europe in the army of Prince Ferdinand of Brunswick. During the war against Napoleonic France it served in the Peninsula and remained there till the end of the war, sharing in the victories of Talavera, Busaco, Almeida and Ciudad Rodrigo; at the siege of the forts of San Vincente, St Cajetano, and La Merced, outside Salamanca; at the Battle of Salamanca and at Burgos, the Pyrenees, the Nivelle, Nive Bayonne, Orthes, Tarbes and Toulouse. Its first battle honour, though, was earned at the Battle of Maida on 4 July 1806 where a small British force under

British soldiers of the 1st Battalion The Gloucestershire Regiment after fighting their way out of a Communist encirclement, pictured on their Bren gun carrier on 9 May 1951.

Major General Sir John Stuart defeated a larger French army in Calabria and in so doing prevented a planned invasion of Sicily. Praising the work of the 61st, the British Minister at Palermo observed that the victory was evidence of 'the superiority of British courage and discipline over an arrogant and cruel enemy'. Such high standards remained with the regiment right to the end. At the final battle of Toulouse, fought on 10 April 1814, the casualties amounted to 20 officers and 161 men killed and wounded. Among the dead was the commanding officer, Lieutenant Colonel Robert Coghlan, and the regiment was left in command of the adjutant, Lieutenant Bace. From the great number of red-coated dead on the field, the 61st gained a proud nickname – 'The Flowers of Toulouse'.

Under the reforms of 1881 the two regiments amalgamated as The Gloucestershire Regiment with two Regular and three Volunteer battalions. The headquarters and depot for the new regiment were situated at Horsfield in Bristol but were relocated after the Second World War to Robinswood Barracks in Gloucester. Both sites have been long since demolished and redeveloped. In 1980 the regimental archives and museum opened in the historic Old Custom House, a handsome building from 1845 that once housed the Collector of Customs and his staff. It was a fitting place to commemorate the regiment as, by long-standing tradition, it drew its recruits from the county of Gloucestershire and from the surrounding area, including Cheltenham, Cirencester, Stroud, Tewkesbury and from the Forest of Dean and Bristol.

During the First World War the Gloucesters raised twenty-five battalions, sixteen of which saw active service, and the regiment was awarded seventy-two battle honours. Two battalions, the 2nd and the 9th, fought in Salonika as part of the forgotten army which found itself in action against Bulgarian forces in this little-remembered campaign. During the fighting in September 1918, a Victoria Cross was awarded to Lieutenant Colonel Daniel Burges of the Gloucesters while he was in temporary command of 7th South Wales Borderers on the Doiran front. Although badly wounded in an attack on Bulgarian positions, the forty-five-year-old from Bristol repeatedly exhorted his men while under heavy fire until he was hit again and fell unconscious. On 24 October 2006, exactly sixty years after his death, a marble plaque to his memory was unveiled in Bristol at Arnos Vale cemetery. Burges's VC was one of six awarded to members of the regiment.

The Gloucestershire Regiment's long life came to an end in 1994 when it amalgamated with The Duke of Edinburgh's Royal Regiment (Berkshire and Wiltshire) to form The Royal Gloucestershire, Berkshire and Wiltshire Regiment. Twelve years later, in 2007, there was further change when the regiment merged with The Devonshire and Dorset Regiment to form the 1st Battalion The Rifles, both regiments having already transferred to the light infantry role.

Although the Gloucesters are no more, the legend of the Imjin River remains a powerful one within the British Army. In 2010, when the headquarters of the NATO Rapid Reaction Corps moved back to the UK from Germany, its new base at RAF Innsworth in Gloucestershire was renamed 'Imjin Lines'.

# Battle Honours

## Pre-1914

*Carried on the Regimental Colour*
**Ramillies, Louisburg, Guadaloupe 1759, Quebec 1759, Martinique 1762, Havannah, St Lucia 1778, Egypt, Maida, Corunna, Talavera, Busaco, Barrosa, Albuhera, Salamanca, Vittoria, Pyrenees, Nivelle, Nive, Orthes, Toulouse, Peninsula, Waterloo, Chillianwallah, Goojerat, Punjaub,Alma, Inkerman, Sevastopol, Delhi 1857, Defence of Ladysmith, Relief of Kimberley, Paardeberg, South Africa 1899–1902**

## First World War (25 battalions)

*Those in bold carried on the Queen's Colour*
**Mons,** Retreat from Mons, Marne 1914, Aisne 1914, 18, **Ypres 1914, 15, 17,** Langemarck 1914, 17, Gheluvelt, Nonne Bosschen, Givenchy 1914, Gravenstafel, St Julien, Frezenberg, Bellewaarde, Aubers, **Loos, Somme 1916, 18,** Albert 1916, 18, Bazentin, Delville Wood, Pozières, Guillemont, Flers-Courcelette, Morval, Ancre Heights, Ancre 1916, Arras 1917, 18, Vimy 1917, Scarpe 1917, Messines 1917, 18, Pilckem, Menin Road, Polygon Wood, Broodseinde, Poelcappelle, Passchendaele, Cambrai 1917, 18, St Quentin, Bapaume 1918, Rosières, Avre, **Lys,** Estaires, Hazebrouck, Bailleul, Kemmel, Béthune, Drocourt-Quéant, Hindenburg Line, Épéhy, Canal du Nord, St Quentin Canal, Beaurevoir, **Selle,** Valenciennes, Sambre, France and Flanders 1914–18, Piave, **Vittorio Veneto,** Italy 1917–18, Struma, **Doiran 1917,** Macedonia 1915–18, Suvla, **Sari Bair,** Scimitar Hill, Gallipoli 1915–16, Egypt 1916, Tigris 1916, Kut al Amara 1917, **Baghdad,** Mesopotamia 1916–18, Persia 1918

## Second World War

*Those in bold carried on the Queen's Colour*
**Defence of Escaut,** St Omer-La-Bassée, Wormhoudt, **Cassel,**
Villers Bocage, **Mont Pincon, Falaise,** Risle Crossing,
Le Havre, Zetten, **North-West Europe 1940, 44–45, Taukyan,**
**Paungde,** Monywa 1942, North Arakan, Mayu Tunnels,
**Pinwe,** Shweli, **Myitson, Burma 1942, 44–45**

## Post-1945 (1st Battalion)

*Carried on the Regimental Colour*
Hill 327, **Imjin, Korea 1950–51**

## Recipients of the Victoria Cross

Surgeon (later Surgeon General) Herbert Taylor Reade,
  61st Regiment, Indian Mutiny, 1857
2nd Lieutenant Hardy Falconer Parsons, 14th Battalion,
  First World War, 1917
Lieutenant Colonel Daniel Burges, The Gloucestershire
  Regiment, Commanding 7th South Wales Borderers,
  First World War, 1918
Captain (later Brigadier) Manley Angell James, 8th Battalion,
  First World War, 1918
Private Francis George Miles, 1/5th Battalion, First World
  War, 1918
Lieutenant Colonel James Power Carne, 1st Battalion,
  Korean War, 1951
Lieutenant Philip Curtis, The Duke of Cornwall's Light
  Infantry, attached 1st Battalion, Korean War, 1951

# The Duke of Wellington's Regiment (West Riding)

## 33rd and 76th

The only line infantry regiment ever to have been named after a commoner, The Duke of Wellington's Regiment also enjoyed close links with the West Riding of Yorkshire. Its depot was situated in Halifax, at Wellesley Barracks in High Road Well, which were vacated in 1959, and the regiment's traditional nickname was 'The Havercake Lads', the havercake being the traditional Yorkshire oat (hafer) cake. A further link with the area was provided by Lieutenant Colonel Edward Akroyd, a local textile manufacturer and a wealthy philanthropist who also commanded the 4th Yorkshire West Riding (Halifax) Rifle Volunteers, which in 1908 became the regiment's Territorial Force battalion. Akroyd died in 1887 after falling from his horse and sustaining severe head injuries but his influence upon the regiment lived on. In 1961 his mansion at Bankfield in Boothtown Road, Halifax, housed the regimental museum which had previously been situated in the old barracks. It was refurbished and extended in 2005.

The regiment was raised in 1702 by Colonel George Hastings, 8th Earl of Huntingdon, who held the first muster near the city of Gloucester at the outbreak of the War of the Spanish Succession. It was immediately in action in continental Europe and was one of six regiments sent to Portugal to help Britain's main ally but it enjoyed mixed fortunes, being almost decimated at the Battle of Almansa in 1707. Re-raised, it took part in the subsequent War of the Austrian Succession where it gained its first battle honour at Dettingen in 1743 and at Roucoux, three years later, it came to public prominence, the *London Gazette* noting that the 33rd Regiment petitioned to attack the enemy and 'did it with so good a countenance that they got a great reputation'. In 1751 the regiment was numbered 33rd in the Army's Order of Precedence and in 1782 it was granted the recruiting area of Yorkshire's West Riding after its Colonel, Lord Cornwallis, informed the War Office that 'the 33rd Regiment of Infantry has always recruited in the West Riding of Yorkshire and has a very good interest and the general goodwill of the people in that part of the county'.

Although it would not have been evident at the time, the most significant change to the 33rd's fortunes came in April 1793 when a young officer, the Hon. Arthur Wellesley, third son of the Earl of Mornington, purchased a major's commission at a cost of £2,600, a sum that would today be worth around £241,900. Four months later he was in command with the rank of lieutenant colonel. With the war against Revolutionary France in full swing there was chance for further advancement and when the 33rd was deployed to India in 1797 Wellesley was determined to make the most of the opportunity, leading them to victory at the Battle of Seringapatam in 1799 in which the forces of Tipu Sultan were defeated. The commanding officer showed that he had his men's interests at heart. He permitted the habit of taking Indian

Group of officers and the Colour Party of 1st Battalion The Duke of Wellington's Regiment, 1896.

mistresses and made sure that the women underwent medical examination, and while he ordered that drunken soldiers be punished he also smiled on officers who drank too heavily, believing that 'the most correct and cautious men were liable to be led astray by convivial society, and no blame ought to attach to an occasional debauch'. Although Wellesley's attachment to the regiment was interrupted by his promotion and return to Britain in 1806, commanding officer and regiment were reunited nine years later when the 33rd formed part of the 5th Brigade in the campaign to defeat Napoleon at Waterloo, masterminded by the Duke of Wellington, as Wellesley had now been created. Thirty-eight years later, on 18 June 1853, following Wellington's death the previous year, Queen Victoria ordered that the regiment's title be changed to The 33rd (The Duke of Wellington's) Regiment in recognition of its long relationship with the great soldier.

By contrast the 76th Regiment of Foot had a more variegated background. It was raised in 1745 at the time of the Jacobite rebellion but was disbanded a year later. Raised again in 1756 at the time of the Seven Years War, it later served in North America as Macdonald's Highlanders before being sent to India in 1787 for service with the Honourable East India Company. For its services George III granted the regiment permission to use the word 'Hindoostan' on its Colours together with an elephant and howdah on its cap badge. The regiment returned to Britain in 1806 and seventy years later shared a depot in Halifax with the 33rd, thus beginning its relationship with the West Riding of Yorkshire. Among its more remarkable officers was John Shipp who was commissioned from the ranks in 1805 but was forced to resign due to lack of funds when the regiment returned to Britain. Nothing daunted, he turned to writing and his *Memoirs*, published in 1827, provide a vivid account of soldiering in the army of the day. He also wrote a treatise against corporal punishment which he argued 'flogged one devil out and fifty devils in'. Many of his suggestions for improvement were adopted by the military authorities.

As a fighting regiment 'The Dukes' (as they quickly became known) had a reputation second to none – it saw action in the Crimea and the Boer War – but it also gained a different kind of fame as one of the army's finest rugby-playing regiments. This began with the 2nd Battalion (the old 76th) which fostered close links with rugby playing schools in Yorkshire and won the first Army Rugby Cup in 1907. Thereafter the regiment won the Army Cup fourteen times and in the 1960s it won the trophy four years in a row. During that sporting heyday the Dukes also produced a number of players who represented their countries at rugby – seven Englishmen, three Scots and one Irishman. Perhaps the best known was M. J. Campbell-Lamerton of Scotland who toured with the British and Irish Lions to South Africa in 1962 and captained them in the following tour to Australia and New Zealand in 1966. The other great Dukes' players were D. W. Shuttleworth and E. M. P. Harding who provided England's half-back partnership in 1951; later, in the rank of brigadier, Shuttleworth was President of the Rugby Football Union during the 1985–86 season.

In common with other regiments the Dukes also profited from the presence of rugby-playing National Servicemen and this also extended to active service. In the

Smiling soldiers of a battalion of The Duke of Wellington's Regiment at the entrance of the shelters they had erected whilst waiting in reserve during the First World War.

period 1952–53 the Dukes were deployed to Korea and took part in the Third Battle of the Hook on the night of 28 May, generally considered to be one of the bloodiest actions of the conflict. It was preceded by a massive Chinese artillery assault and during the following forty-eight hours the Dukes' resistance kept the Hook position secure for the UN forces; even against numerically superior odds, their stoicism and devotion to duty won the day in what was probably the last full-scale defensive infantry battle involving artillery fought by the British Army. Among the Dukes defending the position was nineteen-year-old National Serviceman Lance Corporal Bob Dawson. His recollections are held by the regimental museum: 'The hill we defended was like a lunar landscape, every 5ft trench destroyed and half of the firing pits. As we went to what was left of our hoochies [improvised tarpaulin shelter] at the back of the hill and started to clean our weapons, Major [A. B. M.] Kavanagh came round and said "You are only boys, I hope you never have to go through that again." There were tears in his eyes.' Almost a year later Dawson was back in Yorkshire and demobbed from the army. Not surprisingly he admitted that when he got home he 'felt a complete stranger and it took a long time to settle down'.

Following the 2004 defence review the Dukes became the 3rd Battalion of The Yorkshire Regiment which was formed by The Prince of Wales's Own Regiment of Yorkshire (14th and 15th), The Green Howards (19th) and The Duke of Wellington's Regiment.

# Battle Honours

## Pre-1914

*Carried on the Regimental Colour*
**Hindoostan, Mysore, Seringapatam, Ally Ghur, Delhi 1803, Leswaree, Deig, Corunna, Nive, Peninsular, Waterloo, Alma, Inkerman, Sevastopol, Abyssinia, Relief of Kimberley, Paardeberg, South Africa 1900–02**

## First World War (23 battalions)

*Those in bold carried on the Queen's Colour*
**Mons**, Le Cateau, Retreat from Mons, **Marne 1914, 18**, Aisne 1914, La Bassée 1914, **Ypres 1914, 15, 17**, Nonne Bosschen, **Hill 60**, Gravenstafel, St. Julien, Aubers, **Somme 1916, 18**, Albert 1916 and 1918, Bazentin, Delville Wood, Pozières, Flers-Courcelette, Morval, Thiepval, Le Transloy, Ancre Heights, **Arras 1917, 18**, Scarpe 1917, 18, Arleux, Bullecourt, Messines 1917, 18, Langemarck 1917, Menin Road, Polygon Wood, Broodseinde, Poelcappelle, Passchendaele, **Cambrai 1917, 18**, St Quentin, Ancre 1918, **Lys**, Estaires, Hazebrouck, Bailleul, Kemmel, Bethune, Scherpenberg, Tardenois, Amiens, Bapaume 1918, Drocourt-Quéant, Hindenburg Line, Havrincourt, Épehy, Canal du Nord, Selle, Valenciennes, Sambre, France and Flanders 1914–18, **Piave**, Vittorio Veneto, Italy 1917–18, Suvla, **Landing at Suvla**, Scimitar Hill, Gallipoli 1915, Egypt 1916

## Post-1918

*Carried on the Regimental Colour*
**Afghanistan 1919**

## Second World War

*Those in bold carried on the Queen's Colour*
**Dunkirk, St Valery-en-Caux,** Tilly sur Seulles, Odon, **Fontenay Le Pesnil, North-West Europe 1940, 44–45,** Banana Ridge, Medjez Plain, Gueriat el Atach Ridge, Tunis, **Djebel Bou Aoukaz 1943,** North Africa 1943, **Anzio,** Campoleone, Rome, Monte Ceco, Italy 1943–45, **Sittang 1942,** Paungde, Kohima, Chindits 1944, Burma 1942–44

## Post-1945 (1st Battalion)

*Carried on the Regimental Colour*
The Hook 1953, Korea 1952–53, Iraq 2003

## Recipients of the Victoria Cross

Drummer (later Corporal) Michael Magner, 33rd Regiment, Abyssinia, 1868

Private James Bergin, 33rd Regiment, Abyssinia, 1868

Sergeant James Firth, 1st Battalion, Boer War, 1900

2nd Lieutenant Henry Kelly, 10th Battalion, First World War, 1916

Private Arnold Loosemore, 8th Battalion, First World War, 1917

2nd Lieutenant James Huffam, 5th Battalion, First World War, 1918

Private Arthur Poulter, 1/4th Battalion, First World War, 1918

Private Henry Tandey, 5th Battalion, First World War, 1918

Private Richard Henry Burton, 1st Battalion, Second World War, 1944

# The Border Regiment

## 34th and 55th

The regiment representing the historic region of Cumbria came into being in 1881 as a result of the amalgamation of two distinguished English border county regiments, the 34th (Cumberland) Foot and the 55th (Westmoreland) Foot. Its depot was housed in Carlisle Castle and its character was summed up admirably by the author George MacDonald Fraser who served in the 9th Battalion in Burma in 1944 and whose memoir, *Quartered Safe Out Here* (1992), is one of the best accounts of warfare as experienced by a section of infantrymen. Fraser, the creator of the hugely successful Flashman novels, characterised his fellow Cumbrian soldiers as 'the descendant of one of the hardest breeds of men in Britain, with warfare (if not soldiering) bred into him from the distant past ... in war they were England's vanguard, and in peace her most unruly and bloody nuisance'. It tells us all we need to know about this no-nonsense regiment that its quick march was 'D'ye ken John Peel', the rousing anthem which celebrates the fox-hunting fraternity of the English Border country.

There is no finer example of Fraser's claim about the toughness of Cumbrian soldiers than an incident in October 1811 when the 34th (Cumberland) Foot captured

Farewell parade for Berlin Infantry Brigade commander, March 1959 – men of 1st Battalion The Border Regiment march past. Six months later they amalgamated with The King's Own Royal Regiment (Lancaster) to form The King's Own Royal Border Regiment.

the drums of its opponents at the Battle of Arroyo dos Molinos during the Peninsula campaign against Napoleonic France. To add lustre to the event the six side drums and drum major's staff captured by Sergeant Moses Simpson belonged to the French 34e Regiment and had been presented to them by Napoleon in 1796. This was a signal prize: not only were the 34th (Cumberland) Foot the only regiment to be awarded 'Arroyo dos Molinos' as a battle honour but on each anniversary the drums were paraded by the regiment and its successors. Among those present that day in 1811 was a young ensign from Dublin called George Bell who carried the 34th's King's Colour and who later wrote an entertaining account of his service from young officer to full general. It was his first battle and he never forgot the mixture of elation and fear as he and the colour party began their advance towards the French lines: 'Away we went across the plain to be baptised in blood. Our skirmishers in advance had come across the French outlying pickets and had begun operations. A cannon-shot came rattling past, making a hissing noise, such as I had never heard before. Four sergeants supported the Colours in battle; my old friend [Sergeant] Bolland from Beverley was one of them. I said, "What's that, Bolland?" "Only the morning gun, sir: they're coming on them now." A little onwards and I saw two men cut across by that last shot, the first that I had ever seen killed. I was horrified but said nothing.'

Bell's regiment had been formed over a century earlier when it was raised in East Anglia in February 1702 as Lord Lucas's Regiment of Foot, its founder being Lord Robert Lucas, Governor of the Tower of London.

Originally stationed at Chelmsford, Lucas's Foot was sent north to Carlisle the following year, thereby beginning the lifelong connection between the regiment and the town and its castle. In 1751 it was numbered 34th and in 1782 it was given Cumberland as its territorial title with its depot in Carlisle. During that period it saw service in Europe, the West Indies and Canada, and as Cholmondeley's Regiment it was present in the Duke of Cumberland's army at the Battle of Culloden which ended the Jacobite rebellion of 1745–6. In the nineteenth century the regiment saw action in the wars against Napoleonic France in Europe and India and later in the Crimean War. In 1873 it shared its depot at Carlisle Castle with the 55th (Westmoreland) Foot which had been founded in Stirling in 1755. Raised originally as the 57th Foot it was renumbered two years later following the discovery of irregularities in two line regiments in North America (50th and 51st) leading to their disbandment.

The 55th had the distinction of being one of the few British regiments to have served in China and of having a Chinese dragon superscribed 'China' on its Regimental Colour. This came about in 1841 as a result of the Opium War, a conflict with China over the legalisation of the opium trade: the regiment was part of the invasion force and stayed on in the country as the garrison after the fighting died had down. A Chinese Imperial Dragon Standard flag captured by the 55th at the Battle of Tinghai is held at the Border Regiment Chapel in Kendal Parish Church, together with a pair of Regimental Colours used from 1786 to 1801. After amalgamation the 55th became the 2nd battalion of The Border Regiment and moved to

Men of a battalion of The Border Regiment resting in shallow
dugouts near Thiepval Wood during the Battle of the Somme in
August 1916.

India to replace the 1st Battalion (old 34th) which saw service in the Boer War (1899–1902).

In common with all British line infantry regiments The Border Regiment expanded during the First World War to absorb recruits from the North and North West and five men were awarded the Victoria Cross. The first two won the medal on the same day, 21 December 1914, and in the same action at Rouges Bancs near Armentières when James Alexander Smith and Abraham Acton, of the 2nd Battalion, left their trench to rescue a wounded comrade who had been left in no-man's-land; later that day they repeated the feat to rescue another man, again under heavy enemy fire. Smith was thirty-three and came from Workington; Acton, a twenty-two-year old from Whitehaven, had been a coal miner before the war. Towards the end of the conflict the 2nd Battalion served on the Italian front and gained the battle honour 'Vittoria Veneto' after taking part in that hard-fought battle in 1918.

During the Second World War the 1st Battalion trained for air-landing operations and went into action in Waco gliders pulled by aircraft. The first operation took place during the invasion of Sicily in July 1943 but as Arthur Royall, a young officer who took part in the operation quickly discovered, this was a disastrous undertaking: 'Of the 72 Waco gliders that carried men of The Border Regiment on Operation Ladbroke, one landed in Malta, seven in North Africa, 44 in the sea and only 23 in Sicily – and these were widely scattered. Only 11 officers and 191 ORs actually landed in Sicily.' Before the operation Royall attended a brigade church service and remembered singing the hymn 'Eternal Father, Strong to Save' with the prophetic line 'For those in peril on the sea'. In the following year the same battalion took part in the landings at Arnhem as part of the ill-fated Market Garden operation in September 1944, during which the battalion had a higher casualty rate of dead and wounded than any other in the 1st Airborne Division – only nine officers and 241 other ranks came back after nine days of hard fighting.

In 1959 The Border Regiment amalgamated with its neighbour The King's Own Royal Regiment (Lancaster) to form The King's Own Royal Border Regiment (KORBR). Raised in 1680 as the 2nd Tangier Regiment by the Earl of Plymouth, it became The 4th (King's Own) Regiment in 1751. The territorial connection with Lancaster followed at the time of the Cardwell/Childers reforms and the regimental depot was based at Bowerham Barracks in Lancaster with a recruiting area which ranged from Fleetwood in the south to Barrow-in-Furness in the west and Coniston in the north. On amalgamation with The Border Regiment, Bowerham Barracks were vacated and became the Lancaster Training College (Church of England), and later, the College of St Martin within the University of Cumbria. In 2006 the KORBR amalgamated with The King's Regiment and The Queen's Lancashire Regiment to form The Duke of Lancaster's Regiment (King's, Lancashire and Border).

---

## Battle Honours

### Pre-1914

*Carried on the Regimental Colour*
**Albuhera, Arroyo dos Molinos, Vittoria, Pyrenees, Nivelle, Nive, Orthes, Peninsula, China, Alma, Inkerman, Sevastopol,**

Lucknow, The Relief of Ladysmith 1900, South Africa
1899–1902

## First World War (17 battalions)

*Those in bold carried on the Queen's Colour*
**Ypres 1914, 15, 17, 18, Langemarck 1914, 17,** Gheluvelt,
Neuve Chapelle, Frezenberg, Bellewaarde, Aubers, Festubert
1915, Loos, **Somme 1916, 18,** Albert 1916, 18, Bazentin,
Delville Wood, Pozieres, Guillemont, Flers-Courcelette,
Morval, Thiepval, Le Transloy, Ancre Heights, Ancre 1916,
**Arras 1917, 18,** Scarpe 1917, Bullecourt, Messines 1917, 18
Pilckem, Polygon Wood, Broodseinde, Poelcapelle,
Passchendaele, **Cambrai 1917, 18,** St Quentin, Rosieres, **Lys,**
Estaires, Hazebrouck, Bailleul, Kemmel, Scherpeneberg, Aisne
1918, Amiens, Bapaume 1918, Hindenburg Line, Epehey,
St Quentin Canal, Beuarevoir, Courtrai, Selle, **France and
Flanders 1914–18,** Piave, **Vittorio Veneto,** Italy 1917–18,
**Macedonia 1915–18,** Helles, Landing at Helles, Krithia, Suvla,
Landing at Suvla, Scimitar Hill, **Gallipoli 1916–16,**
Egypt 1916, N.W. Frontier India 1916–17

## Post-1918

*Carried on the Regimental Colour*
**Afghanistan 1919**

## Second World War

*Those in bold carried on the Queen's Colour*
Defence of Escaut, **Dunkirk 1940,** Somme 1940, **Arnhem 1944,
North-West Europe 1940, Tobruk 1941, Landing in Sicily,
Imphal,** Sakawng, Tamu Road, Shenam Pass, Kohima, Ukhrul,
Mandalay, **Myinmu Bridgehead, Meiktila,** Rangoon Road,
Prawbwe, Sittang 1945, **Chindits 1944, Burma 1943–45**

## Recipients of the Victoria Cross

Private John Joseph Sims, 34th Regiment, Crimean War, 1855

Private (later Sergeant) William Coffey, 34th Regiment,
Indian Mutiny, 1857

Brevet Major Frederic Cockayne Elton, 55th Regiment,
Indian Mutiny, 1857

Private (later Sergeant) George Richardson, 34th Regiment,
Indian Mutiny, 1859

Private James Alexander Smith, 2nd Battalion, First World
War, 1914

Private Abraham Acton, 2nd Battalion, First World War, 1914

Sergeant Edward John Mott, 1st Battalion, First World
War, 1917

Sergeant Charles Edward Spackman, 1st Battalion,
First World War, 1917

Captain (Acting Lieutenant Colonel) James Forbes-Robertson
1st Battalion, First World War, 1918

# The Royal Sussex Regiment

## 35th, 107th

The Royal Sussex Regiment possessed all the trappings of a quintessential English county regiment. Its headquarters and depot at Roussillon Barracks were situated in Chichester and through that connection the regiment had an enduring connection with the county of Sussex and its people. However, beneath such orderly traditions the regiment had a rather less settled past. It began life in 1881 as the result of the amalgamation of two very different infantry regiments – the 35th (Royal Sussex) Regiment of Foot and the 107th Bengal Light Infantry Regiment. While it was not uncommon for English regiments to amalgamate with former regiments of the Honourable East India Company, the senior regiment in the partnership had a peripatetic history. It was formed in Ulster in 1701 as the Earl of Donegal's Regiment of Foot, wore orange facings in its uniform and was sometimes referred to as the Belfast Regiment. In 1782, for reasons which have never been explained, it became the 35th (Dorsetshire) Foot and it was not until 1805 that it received Sussex as its territorial designation. The change came about as a result of the influence of Charles Lennox, 4th Duke of Richmond, who had joined the regiment in 1787. Not only did he recruit Sussex men from his family

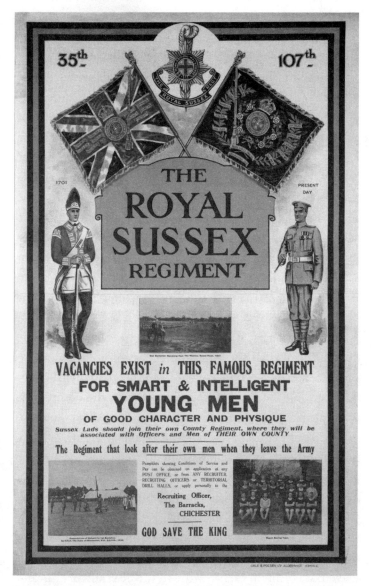

Recruitment poster for The Royal Sussex Regiment, 1929. In time of peace it was difficult to recruit men on ideological grounds alone: this recruitment poster appeals to prospective soldiers' love of sport.

estate at nearby Goodwood but he also obtained George III's permission for the title 'Sussex' to be transferred from the 25th Regiment of Foot to the 35th. (In time the 25th became The King's Own Scottish Borderers.)

Roussillon Barracks remained the regimental home until 1960 when The Royal Sussex moved to Canterbury in Kent and their Chichester home was modernised and extended to become the headquarters of the Royal Military Police. Now part of a housing development following the army's departure in 2005, the barracks occupy a unique place in British military history. In June 1982, following the Falklands War, they provided secure accommodation for Commander Alfredo Astiz, an officer in the Argentine Navy responsible for the invasion of South Georgia, who, before he was repatriated to Argentina in 2011, was the first prisoner of war to be held in Britain since 1945.

Although the 35th was raised for service in Europe during the War of the Spanish Succession it first came to prominence in North America in the 1750s when Britain was fighting the French for possession of the colonies. It was a story that began with disaster and ended in triumph. In the summer of 1757 the 35th was part of a force occupying Fort William Henry, a strategic garrison in the province of New York which was attacked by larger French forces under the command of General Louis-Joseph de Montcalm. Forced to surrender on 9 August, the British commander, Colonel George Forbes, agreed to a surrender which would have allowed the defenders to leave Fort William Henry with all the honours of war and their reputations intact. It was not to be. The Native Americans cared little about European standards of behaviour and promptly set about killing many of the survivors. Despite Montcalm's attempts to restore order and save lives, around two hundred soldiers and camp followers were slaughtered before they could leave Fort William Henry and the 35th was almost wiped out. The incident was vividly portrayed in James Fenimore Cooper's novel *The Last of the Mohicans* (1826).

Two years later the 35th gained their revenge when they were on the right of the army commanded by General James Wolfe at the Battle of the Plains of Abraham fought on 13 September 1759 to capture Quebec. The steady fire of the 35th helped to break the French lines which included the Royal Roussillon Regiment, one of the regiments at Fort William Henry. As the French soldiers fled from the field the 35th advanced and, according to regimental tradition, picked up their white plumes and placed them in their own headdresses. When The Royal Sussex regiment came into being the distinctive Roussillon Plume was incorporated into its badge. The regiment was again in North America during the War of Independence and had the distinction of remaining undefeated throughout three years of fighting. It was honoured with a royal title in 1832, becoming the 35th (Royal Sussex) Foot.

The other regiment in the partnership started life in 1765 as the 3rd Bengal European Regiment which was one of the first to be armed, clothed and drilled in the European fashion. A light infantry title was granted after the Indian Mutiny of 1857 and in 1862 it transferred to the British Army as 107th Regiment (Bengal Light Infantry). Its only Victoria Cross was won by Lieutenant Colonel (later Major General Sir) John Carstairs McNeill, during the invasion of Waikato, a campaign in the Maori

Trumpeters of a battalion of The Royal Sussex Regiment wearing battle dress 'somewhere in England' during the 'Phoney War' in March 1940.

war of 1863–66. A native of the island of Colonsay in the Inner Hebrides, McNeill rescued his orderly from certain death while under heavy enemy fire. After amalgamation with the Royal Sussex, the 107th became the new regiment's 2nd Battalion.

During both the world wars of the twentieth century The Royal Sussex raised additional battalions for operational service on all the main battlefronts – twenty-three in the First World War and fourteen in the Second World War. Perhaps the most poignant action was the Battle of the Boar's Head, a diversionary attack on an obscure salient in the German lines around the tiny village of Richebourg-l'Avoué in northern France, which is barely mentioned in any of the war histories. It was fought on 30 June 1916, the day before the Battle of the Somme began, and it involved three Royal Sussex battalions, the 11th, 12th and 13th, all 'South Downs Pals' from the same county who were going into the attack for the first time.

Following the usual bombardment of the German trenches, the 12th and 13th Battalions went into the attack and immediately faced heavy German machine-gun fire. Supported by the 11th Battalion they succeeded in taking the German front line trench, holding it for some five hours. During this phase of the fighting Company Sergeant Major Nelson Victor Carter from Hailsham rallied his men and would later be awarded a posthumous Victoria Cross. Before the war he worked as a commissionaire at the Old Town Cinema in Eastbourne, the first in the town, and there is a blue plaque in his memory at his home at 33 Greys Road.

Only steadily mounting casualties and a shortage of ammunition forced the men of the three South Downs battalions to retire but their cussedness came at a terrible price: they lost 17 officers and 349 men killed with almost a thousand more wounded or taken prisoner. Among the casualties were twelve sets of brothers; one family lost three sons. With good reason this unnecessary battle was memorialised as 'The Day Sussex Died'.

One of the officers present was Edmund Blunden who served in the 11th Battalion and later became a leading war poet. In his memoir *Undertones of War* he quoted a sentry who responded to a general's query about the battle by saying, 'It was like a butcher's shop.' The other notable writer associated with the regiment was Richard Aldington whose autobiographical novel, *Death of Hero*, is one of the great novels of the First World War.

On 31 December 1966 the regiment was amalgamated with other Home Counties regiments to form The Queen's Regiment. Further changes came in 1992 when The Queen's amalgamated with The Royal Hampshire Regiment to form The Princess of Wales's Royal Regiment. On amalgamation the Regimental Colours were laid up in Chichester Cathedral. For a flavour of what a traditional English county regiment represented it is worth visiting The Royal Sussex Regimental Museum at the Eastbourne Redoubt in Eastbourne, built on the site of Napoleonic Wars coastal defences.

# Battle Honours

## Pre-1914

*Carried on the Regimental Colour*
**Gibraltar 1704–05, Louisburg, Quebec 1759, Martinique 1762, Havannah, St. Lucia 1778, Maida, Egypt 1882, Abu Klea, Nile 1884–85, South Africa 1900–02**

## First World War (23 battalions)

Mons, **Retreat from Mons, Marne 1914**, 18, Aisne 1914, **Ypres 1914, 17, 18, Gheluvelt**, Nonne Bosschen, Givenchy 1914, Aubers, Loos, **Somme 1916, 18**, Albert 1916, 18, Bazentin, Delville Wood, Pozières, Flers-Courcelette, Morval, Thiepval, Le Transloy, Ancre Heights, Ancre 1916, 18, Arras 1917, 18, Vimy 1917, Scarpe 1917, Arleux, Messines 1917, **Pilckem**, Langemarck 1917, Menin Road, Polygon Wood, Broodseinde, Poelcappelle, Passchendaele, Cambrai 1917, 18, St. Quentin, Bapaume 1918, Rosières, Avre, Lys, Kemmel, Scherpenberg, Soissonais-Ourcq, Amiens, Drocourt-Quéant, **Hindenburg Line**, Épéhy, St. Quentin Canal, Beaurevoir, Courtrai, Selle, Sambre, France and Flanders 1914–18, Piave, Vittorio Veneto, **Italy 1917–18**, Suvla, Landing at Suvla, Scimitar Hill, **Gallipoli 1915**, Rumani, Egypt 1915–17, Gaza, El Mughar, Jerusalem, Jericho, Tell 'Asur, **Palestine 1917–18, N.W. Frontier India 1915, 1916–17**, Murman 1918–19

## Post-1918

*Carried on the Regimental Colour*
**Afghanistan 1919**

## Second World War

*Those in bold carried on the Queen's Colour*
Defence of Escaut, Amiens 1940, St. Omer-La Bassée, Forêt de
Nieppe, **North-West Europe 1940**, Karora-Marsa Taclai,
Cub Cub, Mescelit Pass, Keren, Mt. Engiahat, Massawa,
**Abyssinia 1941, Omars**, Benghazi, **Alam el Halfa, El Alamein,
Akarit**, Djebel el Meida, Tunis, **North Africa 1940–43,
Cassino I**, Monastery Hill, Gothic Line, Pian di Castello,
Monte Reggiano, **Italy 1944–45**, North Arakan, Pinwe,
Shweli, **Burma 1943–45**

## Recipients of the Victoria Cross

Lieutenant Colonel (later Major General) John Carstairs
   McNeill, 107th Regiment, Maori War, 1864
Sergeant Harry Wells, 2nd Battalion, First World War, 1915
Lieutenant Eric McNair, 9th Battalion, First World War, 1916
Company Sergeant Major Nelson Carter, 12th Battalion,
   First World War, 1916
Lieutenant Colonel (later Major General) Dudley Johnson,
   The South Wales Borderers, Commanding 2nd Royal
   Sussex, First World War, 1918
Captain Lionel Ernest Queripel, The Royal Sussex Regiment,
   attached 10th Parachute Regiment, Second World War, 1944

# The South Staffordshire Regiment

## 38th and 80th

Staffordshire's senior county regiment was formed in 1881 as a result of the amalgamation of the 38th (1st Staffordshire) Foot and the 80th (Staffordshire Volunteers) Foot. From the outset the new regiment enjoyed strong links with the county and wore a cap badge that incorporated the traditional Staffordshire three-looped knot, which is also the symbol of the Earls of Stafford. It also began the tradition of having a Staffordshire bull terrier as a mascot. The first was called Boxer. He accompanied the regiment to Egypt and survived a solitary 200-mile trek across the Sudanese desert after leaping from a train and being left for dead while the regiment was being taken south as part of the force to relieve General Gordon in Khartoum in 1885. This extraordinary feat encouraged the South Staffords and its successor regiment to have a Staffordshire bull terrier mascot with its own rank of sergeant. After 1949 the dog's official name was Watchman.

The South Staffords' story began in 1705 when General Luke Lillingstone raised a regiment of foot using as his headquarters the King's Head, in Bird Street, Lichfield, thereby beginning a lifelong association with the county of Staffordshire. The pub is still there under the same name but no longer has any official connection with the regiment. In the early years the regiment was known as Lillingstone's Regiment of Foot; it received the number 38th in 1751 and the Staffordshire territorial connection was added in 1782. Shortly after its foundation, Lillingstone took his regiment to the West Indies, an unpopular posting because of the unhealthy climate and the distance from home. For most of the time it was based on the island of Antigua and it remained there until 1764, making this the longest overseas posting of any regiment in the British Army. It was not an easy time. In addition to the high death toll, clothing wore out very quickly and the only alternative material to make tropical uniforms came from the sacking to store sugar. This unusual improvisation was commemorated in the 'Holland Patch' of coarse sacking worn behind the cap badge and on the collar badges of the South Staffordshire Regiment.

On amalgamation the 38th became the new regiment's 1st Battalion while the younger 80th became its 2nd Battalion. Immediately thereafter the 1st Battalion was sent to Egypt in 1882 as part of the British invasion of the country to restore order following a *coup d'état* which unseated the Khedive Tewfik Pasha, a key British ally. On landing in Alexandria, 1st South Staffords marched its Regimental Colours through the city, the last time a British regiment would take such action on active service. Three years later, in 1885, the battalion travelled up the River Nile to Sudan in an unsuccessful attempt to relieve Khartoum and rescue General Gordon. It was subsequently involved in the defeat of Arab forces at Kirbekan and that battle was to be the last time that the South Staffords wore red uniforms in combat, a distinction it shares with

The Mayor of Walsall presenting new drums to 5th Battalion
The South Staffordshire Regiment in July 1925.

1st Black Watch, which also took part in the engagement. There was only one casualty in the Staffords – that of the commanding officer, Lieutenant Colonel Philip Eyre, whose death is commemorated by a brass plaque in the north wall of Lichfield Cathedral.

The other constituent battalion was the 80th (Staffordshire Volunteers) Foot which was raised on 9 December 1793 by Lord Henry Paget, later 1st Marquess of Anglesey. Most of the men came from the local Staffordshire Volunteers or were recruited from the estates of Paget's father at Beaudesert on the edge of Cannock Chase in Staffordshire. The estate was broken up and sold in 1935 and the elegant Elizabethan brick mansion house demolished. During the course of the nineteenth century the 80th Foot served in India and Africa and was part of Lord Chelmsford's army which suffered defeat at Isandlwana in the Zulu War of 1879. Out of this disaster came the second of the regiment's two Victoria Crosses, awarded to Private Samuel Wassall, a native of Dudley, Staffordshire, who saved a fellow soldier from drowning in the Buffalo River while both men were being threatened by the presence of the enemy. On reaching the bank the two men mounted Wassall's horse and made good their escape. Before his death at Barrow-in-Furness in 1927, married and the father of seven children, Wassall recorded his memory of that dramatic moment: 'At this time I was very lightly cold, I had thrown my helmet aside and my red tunic off, the British soldiers fought in the good old red in those days and not in khaki, so that I was clothed in just my shirt and trousers with my bandolier over my shirt and so I rode on as hard as I could, with a few of the fugitives from Isandlwana.'

Given the South Staffords' long fighting history it is not surprising that it has produced several outstanding battlefield commanders. In addition to Lord Paget of the 80th, who ended his career as a field marshal, there was General Lord Rowland Hill who was commissioned in the 38th Regiment in 1791 and also served in the 90th Perthshire Light Infantry. (See The Cameronians.) Hill fought with Wellington in the Peninsula and at Waterloo and although he eventually became the army's commander-in-chief he never lost the common touch. Renowned throughout the army for his gentleness and consideration to soldiers, 'Daddy' Hill once provided a sergeant with a meal and a bed for the night after he had delivered an important despatch, unusual behaviour from a senior officer at the time.

During the Second World War both the regular battalions of the South Staffords found themselves undertaking unfamiliar roles. The 1st Battalion fought in Burma as part of Orde Wingate's Chindits and had to be trained in the rigours of jungle warfare and fighting behind enemy lines. At the same time the 2nd Battalion was trained as an air-landing force going into battle by glider and served in the campaigns in Sicily in 1943, and at Arnhem in 1944 where losses were high. The battalion set out with an operational strength of 867, but only 139 survived to return to British lines. During the fighting two South Staffords were awarded the Victoria Cross – both Major Robert Henry Cain and Lance Sergeant John Daniel Baskeyfield displayed incredible bravery while engaging German armoured vehicles in separate incidents. Baskeyfield was killed in action and his body was never found but he is commemorated by a statue at Festival

Soldiers of the South Staffordshire Regiment serving with the
2nd Division guard a road with a Bren gun during a military training
operation in England in 1936.

Heights in Stoke-on-Trent, which was unveiled in 1990. The full extent of Major Cain's courage was only revealed to his daughter Frances after his death. According to her husband, the motoring journalist and broadcaster Jeremy Clarkson, who made a television documentary on prominent VC winners in 2003, 'he'd never thought to mention it' (Major Cain was commissioned in The Royal Northumberland Fusiliers).

In 1959 the South Staffords amalgamated with the neighbouring North Staffordshire Regiment (The Prince of Wales's) to become The Staffordshire Regiment (Prince of Wales's). For many years the regimental museum was in Davidson House in St John's Street, Lichfield, but today it is housed in a modern purpose-built structure in Whittington Barracks, three miles from Lichfield and the regimental depot of both constituent regiments since 1880. The Staffords remained in existence until 2007 when it became the 3rd Battalion of The Mercian Regiment, a new large regiment formed by an amalgamation of The Cheshire Regiment (22nd), The Worcester and Sherwood Foresters (29th and 45th) and the Staffords. As a result of the 2010 defence review the regiment's 3rd Battalion was earmarked for disbandment in 2014 following a final tour of duty in Afghanistan.

---

## Battle Honours

### Pre-1914

*Carried on the Regimental Colour*
**Guadeloupe 1759, Martinique 1762, Rolica, Vimiera,**

Corunna, Busaco, Badajos, Salamanca, Vittoria, St Sebastian, Nive, Peninsula, Ava, Moodkee, Ferozeshah, Sobraon, Pegu, Alma, Inkerman, Sevastopol, Lucknow, Central India, South Africa 1878–79, Egypt 1882, Kirbekan, Nile 1884–85, South Africa 1900–02

## First World War (18 battalions)

*Those in bold carried on the Queen's Colour*
**Mons,** Retreat from Mons, **Marne, 1914, Aisne, 1914, 18, Ypres, 1914, 17,** Langemarck 1914, 17, Gheluvelt, Nonne Boschen, Neuve Chapelle, Aubers, Festubert 1915, **Loos, Somme, 1916, 18,** Albert 1916, 18, Bazentin, Delville Wood, Pozieres, Flers-Courcelette, Morval, Thiepval, Ancre 1916, Bapaume 1917, 18, Arras 1917, 18, Scarpe 1917, 18, Arleux, Bullecourt, Hill 70, Messine 1917, 18, Menin Road, Polygon Wood, Broodseinde, Poelcapelle, Passchendaele, **Cambrai, 1917, 18,** St Quentin, Lys, Bailleul, Kemmel, Scherpenberg, Droucourt-Queant, Hindenburg Line, Havrincourt, Canal du Nord, **St Quentin Canal,** Beaurevoir, Selle, Sambre, France and Flanders 1914–18, **Vittorio Veneto,** Italy 1917–18, **Suvla,** Landing at Suvla, Scimitar Hill, Gallipoli 1915, Egypt 1916

## Second World War

*Those in bold carried on the Queen's Colour*
**Caen, Noyers, Falaise, Arnhem 1944, North-West Europe 1940, 44,** Sidi Barrani, **North Africa 1940, Landing in Sicily, Sicily, 1943,** Italy 1943, **Chindits 1944, Burma 1944**

## Recipients of the Victoria Cross

Private Samuel Wassall, 80th Regiment, Zulu War, 1879
Colour Sergeant Anthony Clarke Booth, 80th Regiment,
 Zulu War, 1879

Captain John Franks Vallentin, 1st Battalion, First World War, 1914

Captain Arthur Forbes Gordon Kilby, 2nd Battalion, First World War, 1915

Private Thomas Barratt, 7th Battalion, First World War, 1917

Lance Sergeant John Daniel Baskeyfield, 2nd Battalion, Second World War, 1944

Major Robert Henry Cain, The Royal Northumberland Fusiliers, attached 2nd South Staffordshire Regiment, Second World War, 1944

# The Oxfordshire and Buckinghamshire Light Infantry

## 43rd and 52nd

Known affectionately to generations of soldiers as 'The Ox and Bucks', the regiment combined the histories of two distinguished light infantry regiments from very different geographical locations. In 1741 the 43rd was raised as Thomas Fowke's Regiment of Foot, becoming the 43rd (Monmouthshire Foot) in 1782, while the 52nd was raised in 1755 and was later associated with the county of Oxfordshire. Both received the Light Infantry title in 1803 as a result of being chosen to join the newly formed Light Infantry Brigade, an elite formation which also included the 95th, later The Rifle Brigade. Its commander was Major General Sir John Moore of the 52nd who was regarded by his contemporaries as 'the very best trainer of troops that England has ever possessed'. He was mortally wounded during the retreat to Corunna in 1809 and his last words were an appeal to posterity: 'I hope the people of England will be satisfied! I hope my country will do me justice!'

During the fighting in the Peninsula against the army of Napoleon, light infantry regiments came into their own as skirmishers and sharpshooters and, with their smart green uniforms and bugle horn cap badges, the 'light bobs' (as they were known) were exceptionally

Recruitment poster for the Oxfordshire and Buckinghamshire Light printed by Gale and Polden Limited of Aldershot in 1920.

proud of their reputations. From the outset the 43rd and the 52nd enjoyed a close relationship, one observer noting that the soldiers of the 52nd were 'highly gentlemanly men, of steady aspect; they mixed little with other corps, but attended the theatricals of the 43rd with circumspect good humour, and now and then relaxed'.

At the time of Waterloo the 43rd was part of an expeditionary force sent to North America and took part in the disastrous Battle of New Orleans before returning to Europe. It therefore missed the heroic attack of the 52nd during the closing stages of Waterloo when it came to the aid of the Grenadier Guards by enfilading the 4th Chasseurs and pursuing French forces across the field. A watching ensign, William Leeke, later wrote a history of Waterloo and believed that this was the pivotal moment in the battle: 'The author claims for Lord Seaton [Sir John Colburn, the commanding officer] and the 52nd the honour of having defeated, single-handed, without the assistance of the 1st British Guards or any other troops, that portion of the Imperial Guard of France, about 10,000 in number, which advanced to make the last attack on the British position.'

After the two regiments amalgamated in 1881 to form the 1st and 2nd Battalions of The Oxfordshire Light Infantry it was only natural that neighbouring Buckinghamshire should be added to the title twenty-seven years later in recognition of the volunteer battalions within the county. Their records and archives are housed in the Buckinghamshire Military Museum at the Old Gaol Museum in Buckingham. However, the new regiment's depot was at Cowley Barracks at Headington in Oxford. These closed in 1959 and the site was used as

The officers of the 52nd (Oxfordshire and Buckinghamshire) Light Infantry and reception committee on the occasion of the battalion's visit to Chipping Norton on 27 September 1913.

the headquarters of the United Kingdom Warning and Monitoring Organisation which was responsible for providing the famous 'four-minute warning' in the case of imminent nuclear attack during the Cold War. Today it forms part of the site of Oxford Brookes University.

Given the regiment's hinterland it is not surprising that many of its soldiers enjoyed close links with academia. Among the most notable were the leading oarsman Frank Willan, the Vice-Chancellor (1958–60) of the University of Oxford, T. S. R. Boase, and the radical historian Christopher Hill. Of these Willan rowed in the winning Oxford eight for four successive years between 1866 and 1869 and at well over seventy was still employed driving army lorries in France during the First World War. Boase was awarded a Military Cross while serving in the regiment on the Western Front and went on to become director of the Courtauld Institute before serving as a code-breaker at Bletchley Park during the Second World War. An outstanding historian of seventeenth-century Britain, Hill became disenchanted with the Communist Party in the late 1950s and eventually became Master of Balliol College. Other notable Ox and Bucks Light Infantrymen include the actor and director Lionel Jeffries, who directed the highly popular film *The Railway Children* (1970), and General Sir Bernard Paget, Commander-in-Chief of Middle East Command in the final years of the Second World War.

As with all regiments of the British Army, the Ox and Bucks expanded dramatically during the First World War, raising seventeen battalions for service, and it was one of the few infantry regiments to serve on most of the main battlefronts – France and Flanders, Italy, Salonika and

Mesopotamia (modern Iraq). During the Second World War the 2nd Battalion fought in an air-landing role and June 1944 played a vital part in the D-Day landings by capturing the bridges over the River Orne and the Caen Canal on the first night of the operation. Led by Major John Howard, D Company was flown in by gliders towed by Halifax bombers and after a fierce fire fight seized their objectives. Although Lieutenant Den Brotheridge was mortally wounded during the attack, thereby becoming the first Allied casualty of D-Day, the operation was a stunning success and later the two bridges were renamed Pegasus Bridge, in honour of the airborne forces, and Horsa Bridge, after the gliders which flew in the airborne light infantrymen. In the film *The Longest Day*, based on a history of the operation by Cornelius Ryan, the part of Major Howard was played by the distinguished British actor Richard Todd who had actually served in 7th Parachute Battalion, which reinforced D Company's *coup de main*. Later in the invasion of Europe, 2nd Oxfordshire and Buckinghamshire Light Infantry again operated in the air-landing role during the Rhine crossings where they suffered heavy casualties – all told, the battalion lost 1408 officers and men in the course of the conflict. The 1st Battalion also took part in the invasions of Europe and the other Ox and Bucks battalions involved in the fighting were the 6th Battalion, which was engaged in the fighting against the Japanese in Burma, and the 7th Battalion, which fought in North Africa and Italy.

Throughout the regiment's history the Ox and Bucks enjoyed many distinctions that marked them out as an elite force. In common with all rifle regiments they did not carry Colours and used the bugle instead of the drum to transmit orders; and instead of wearing a leather Sam Browne belt across the right shoulder, officers wore two straps crossed in the middle of the back and running straight down the front from shoulder to shoulder. The regiment's archives and records are held by the Soldiers of Oxfordshire Museum at Woodstock within the grounds of the Oxfordshire Museum.

On 7 November 1958 the regiment became the 1st Battalion of The Green Jackets and moved to Peninsula Barracks in Winchester. This was followed by further change in 1966 when it became the 1st Battalion of the newly formed three-battalion Royal Green Jackets regiment. In 1992 1st Battalion Royal Green Jackets was disbanded but the traditions and historical lineage of the Ox and Bucks have been maintained by The Rifles which came into being in 2007 through the amalgamation of the army's light infantry and rifle regiments. The last ever Royal Green Jackets unit was the London Oratory School Combined Cadet Force which was rebadged as Irish Guards in 2010.

---

## Battle Honours

### Pre-1914

*Carried on the Regimental Colour*
**Quebec 1759, Martinique 1762, Havannah, Mysore, Hindoostan, Martinique 1794, Vimiera, Corunna, Busaco, Fuentes d'Onor, Ciudad Rodrigo, Badajoz, Salamanca, Vittoria, Pyrenees, Nivelle, Nive, Orthes, Toulouse, Peninsula, Waterloo, South Africa 1851–2–3, Delhi 1857, New Zealand, Relief of Kimberley, Paardeberg, South Africa 1900–02**

## First World War (17 battalions)

*Those in bold carried on the Queen's Colour*
**Mons**, Retreat from Mons, Marne 1914, Aisne 1914, **Ypres 1914, 17, Langemarck 1914, 17**, Gheluvelt, **Nonne Bosschen**, Aubers, Festubert 1915, Hooge 1915, Loos, Mount Sorrel, **Somme 1916, 18**, Albert 1916, 18, Bazentin, Delville Wood, Poziéres, Guillemont, Flers-Courcelette, Morval, Le Transloy, Ancre Heights, Ancre 1916, Bapaume 1917, 18, Arras 1917, Vimy 1917, Scarpe 1917, Arleux, Menin Road, Polygon Wood, Broodseinde, Poelcapelle, Passchendaele, **Cambrai 1917, 18**, St Quentin, Rosiéres, Avre, Lys, Hazebrouck, Béthune, Hindenburg Line, Havrincort, Canal du Nord, Selle, Valenciennes, France and Flanders 1914–18, **Piave**, Vittorio Veneto, Italy 1917–18, **Doiran 1917, 18**, Macedonia 1915–18, Kut-al-Amara, **Ctesiphon, Defence of Kut-al-Amara**, Tigris 1916, Khan Baghdadi, Mesopotamia 1914–18, Archangel 1919

## Second World War

*Those in bold carried on the Queen's Colour*
Defence of Escaut, **Cassel, Ypres-Comines-Canal, Normandy Landing, Pegasus Bridge**, Caen, Esquay, Lower Maas, Ourthe, Rhineland, **Reichswald, Rhine**, Ibbenbüren, North-West Europe 1940, 44–45, **Enfidaville**, North Africa 1943, **Salerno**, St Lucia, Salerno Hills, Teano, Monte Camino, Garigliano Crossing, Damiano, **Anzio**, Coriano, **Gemmano Ridge**, Italy 1943–45, Arakan Beaches, Tamandu, Burma 1943–45

## Recipients of the Victoria Cross

Company Sergeant Major Edward Brooks, 2/4th Battalion, First World War, 1917
Lance Corporal Alfred Wilcox, 2/4th Battalion, First World War, 1918

# The Essex Regiment

## 44th and 56th

If one painting sums up the selfless heroism and devotion to duty which underpinned Queen Victoria's army it is William Barnes Wollen's 'The Last Stand of the 44th Regiment at Gundamuck'. Although it is a sanitised and highly romanticised interpretation of one of the worst disasters to befall a British army during the First Afghan War (1839–42), it remains a heroic vision of how soldiers will behave *in extremis* and when they have only their courage and pride in regiment to sustain them. The bare facts speak for themselves. In 1839 British and Indian forces had invaded Afghanistan and effected a regime change in order to protect British interests in the region but within three years had been forced to withdraw. During the retreat back to India from Kabul through the snowbound passes, most of the 16,500-strong force was massacred, leaving the depleted 44th (East Essex) Foot to make a last stand on a rocky hill near the village of Gandamak. Only sixty-five men of Essex remained in position in their small defensive square; they had little ammunition and were exhausted and freezing but national pride was at stake. When the Afghans called on them to surrender a sergeant's voice was heard crying out, 'Not bloody likely!' Only two men survived – Captain

Thomas Souter, who wrapped the Regimental Colour around him before being taken prisoner, and Surgeon William Brydon, who managed to ride back to India with news of the disaster. Wollen's painting now hangs in the Chelmsford and Essex Museum in Oaklands Park, London Road, Chelmsford.

Gandamak was not the first time the Essex infantrymen had been annihilated in battle; to the 44th belongs the unhappy statistic of being wiped out on three different occasions during its first hundred years of service to the Crown. The regiment was one of seven raised in 1741 to fight in the War of the Austrian Succession and it was originally known as Long's Regiment after its first Colonel, James Long of the Grenadier Guards. Four years later, as Lee's Regiment, its new Colonel being John Lee, it was part of the government army which faced rebel Jacobite forces at Prestonpans outside Edinburgh on 21 September 1745. Unable to withstand the ferocity of the Highlanders' charge, the government infantry broke and fled from the field only to be savagely cut down by the pursuing clansmen. Among those killed were the men of Lee's Regiment.

Almost ten years later, on 9 July 1755, the same regiment, by then numbered the 44th, was massacred by French and Native Americans while serving under Major General Edward Braddock in North America. During the fighting on the Monongahela River in modern western Pennsylvania, sixty-three British and American officers were killed and wounded while the casualties among the NCOs and men were 914, many of them from the 44th. Undaunted by their experience the regiment re-formed and served in North America throughout the War of

Soldiers of the Essex Regiment ferried across the River Vaal in
South Africa during the Boer War 1899–1902. Both the 1st and 2nd
Battalions saw action during the conflict.

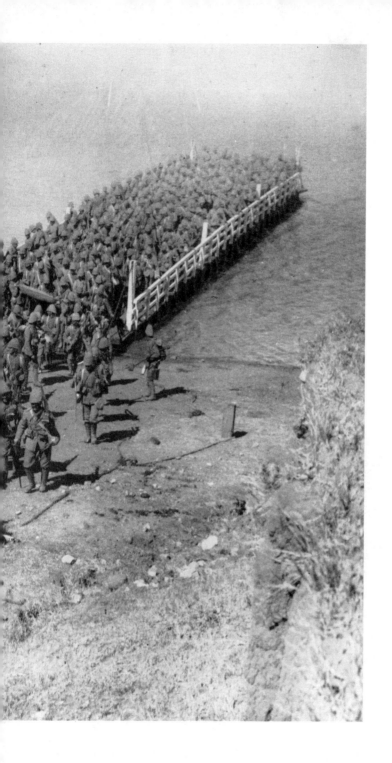

Independence, seeing action at the battles of Brooklyn (1776), Brandywine (1777) and Monmouth (1778). As if to compensate for its earlier setbacks the 44th gained great glory during the Peninsular War when its newly raised 2nd Battalion captured a French imperial eagle – the equivalent of a British regiment's Colours – at the Battle of Salamanca which was fought on 22 July 1812. It was one of only five such eagles to be captured and the deed earned the 2nd Battalion the nickname 'the little fighting fours'.

In 1881 as part of the reform of the infantry system the 44th amalgamated with the 56th (West Essex) Foot to form The Essex Regiment with its depot and headquarters at Warley, now a suburb of Brentwood. Little remains of the site, which was developed by the Ford Motor Company as its British headquarters; the only vestiges are the officers' mess (now the Marillac Nursing Home) and one of the regimental gyms (Keys Hall). However, the area is still home to the handsome Essex Regimental Chapel in Eagle Way (built in 1857) and contains many historical artefacts, including the regiment's Colours. On amalgamation with the 56th Foot the new regiment adopted its nickname 'The Pompadours', a reference to its purple facings which were changed from deep red in 1764. Why the colour was so called remains a mystery; it has been claimed that purple was the favourite colour of Louis XV's mistress and confidante Madame de Pompadour, but within the regiment itself soldiers preferred to say that the nickname came from the colour of her underwear. A more reliable tradition was the use of 'Rule, Britannia!' as The Essex Regiment's quick march to commemorate the 56th's service as marines on board the frigates HMS *Psyche* and HMS *Piedmontaise* between 1809 and1810.

During the First World War the regiment raised thirty-one battalions, eleven of which saw action on that conflict's main battlefronts. However, the regiment was closely associated with the ill-fated Gallipoli campaign in 1915, providing the invasion force with not only the 1st Battalion in the 'Immortal' 29th Division but also four Territorial battalions which served together in the 161st Essex Brigade. First into action was 1st Essex which landed at W Beach on 25 April and suffered heavy casualties as it attacked Turkish positions on Hill 138 supported by 4th Worcester Regiment. Among the hundred or so casualties that day was Private John Edwin Barnes, a regular who was typical of the pre-war infantry soldier who joined up out of a sense of adventure and to break the tedium of civilian life in England. Born in Poplar in 1890, he enlisted at eighteen and served with 2nd Essex in Dublin before being posted to India to serve with the 1st Battalion. At the other end of the scale is the well-attested case of a Private Stacey from Warley who enlisted in The Essex Regiment in 1902 at the age of only fifteen. After discovering that his kit had been stolen and sold off while he was on leave (a common occurrence) Stacey deserted and walked from Warley to Reading where he enlisted in The Berkshire Regiment under the name Charles Cotton. When his cover was about to be broken by the appearance of two other men from The Essex Regiment he deserted once again and rejoined the army at Aldershot where he enlisted in The King's Royal Rifle Corps. Five months later he was on the move again, enlisting in The Royal West Kent Regiment at Gravesend, again under an assumed name.

Soldiers of the Essex Regiment recuperating at Queen Mary's Orthopaedic Hospital, Roehampton, London, a specialised orthopaedic hospital established during the First World War. One of a series of contemporary postcards.

Following the failure of the Gallipoli campaign at the end of 1915 the regiment's four Territorial battalions (4th, 5th, 6th and 7th) served in Egypt and Palestine but the 1st Battalion returned with the 29th Division to France where it saw service on the Western Front and was in action on the first day of the Somme, 1 July 1916, at Beaumont-Hamel. Its task was to support The Newfoundland Regiment as it went into the attack shortly after nine o'clock in the morning, only to suffer some 710 casualties in the resulting firestorm. Two hours later 1st Essex began its attack but it quickly became bogged down in no-man's-land, leaving the commanding officer with no option but to inform brigade headquarters that the battalion had to withdraw 'owing to casualties and disorganisation'. On the Thiepval Memorial, which commemorates the dead of the Somme, are the names of 949 officers and men of The Essex Regiment who have no known grave.

During the Second World War Essex battalions served in Europe and Burma but the regiment did not long survive the peace. In 1958 it amalgamated with The Bedfordshire and Hertfordshire Regiment to form the 3rd Battalion of The East Anglian Regiment, which became The Royal Anglian Regiment in 1964. In 1992 the 3rd Battalion was disbanded but the Essex connection is maintained by the Corps of Drums at King Edward VI Grammar School at Chelmsford, which uses the drums of the old 4th/5th Battalion and wears scarlet tunics with Pompadour purple facings.

# Battle Honours

## Pre-1914

*Carried on the Regimental Colour*
**Egypt, Moro, Gibraltar 1779–83, Badajoz, Salamanca,
Peninsula, Bladensburg, Waterloo, Ava, Alma, Inkerman,
Sevastopol, Taku Forts, Havannah, Nile 1884–85, Relief
of Kimberley, Paardeberg, South Africa 1899–1902**

## First World War (31 battalions)

*Those in bold carried on the Queen's Colour*
**Le Cateau**, Retreat from Mons, **Marne 1914**, Aisne 1914,
Messines 1914, Armentières 1914, **Ypres 1915, 17**, St. Julien,
Frezenberg, Bellewaarde, **Loos, Somme 1916, 18**, Albert 1916,
18, Bazentin, Delville Wood, Pozières, Flers-Courcelette,
Morval, Thiepval, Le Transloy, Ancre Heights, Ancre 1916,
18, Bapaume 1917, 18, **Arras 1917, 18**, Scarpe 1917, 18,
Arleux, Pilckem, Langemarck 1917, Menin Road,
Broodseinde, Poelcappelle, Passchendaele, **Cambrai 1917, 18**,
St. Quentin, Avre, Villers Bretonneux, Lys, Hazebrouck,
Béthune, Amiens, Drocourt-Quéant, Hindenburg Line,
Havrincourt, Épéhy, St. Quentin Canal, **Selle**, Sambre, France
and Flanders 1914–18, Helles, Landing at Helles, Krithia,
Suvla, Landing at Suvla, Scimitar Hill, **Gallipoli 1915–16**,
Rumani, Egypt 1915–17, **Gaza**, Jaffa, Megiddo, Sharon,
Palestine 1917–18

## Second World War

*Those in bold carried on the Queen's Colour*
St. Omer-La Bassée, Tilly sur Seulles, Le Havre, Antwerp-
Turnhout Canal, Scheldt, **Zetten**, Arnhem 1945, **North-West
Europe 1940, 44–45**, Abyssinia 1940, Falluja, Baghdad 1941,
Iraq 1941, **Palmyra**, Syria 1941, **Tobruk 1941**, Belhamed,

Mersa Matruh, **Defence of Alamein Line,** Deir el Shein, Ruweisat, Ruweisat Ridge, El Alamein, Matmata Hills, Akarit, **Enfidaville,** Djebel Garci, Tunis, Ragoubet Souissi, North Africa 1941–43, Trigno, **Sangro, Villa Grande, Cassino I,** Castle Hill, Hangman's Hill, Italy 1943–44, Athens, Greece 1944–45, Kohima, **Chindits 1944,** Burma 1943–45

## Recipients of the Victoria Cross

Sergeant William McWheeney, 44th Regiment, Crimean
  War, 1854
Private (later Sergeant) John McDougall, 44th Regiment,
  Second Opium War 1860
Lieutenant (later Major General) Robert Montresor Rogers,
  44th Regiment, Second Opium War, 1860
Lieutenant Francis Newton Parsons, 1st Battalion, Boer
  War, 1900
2nd Lieutenant Frank Bernard Wearne, 11th Battalion,
  First World War, 1917
Lieutenant Colonel Augustus Charles Newman, The Essex
  Regiment, attached 2 Commando, Second World War, 1942

# The Sherwood Foresters (Nottinghamshire and Derbyshire Regiment)

## 45th and 95th

Perhaps the most romantically named of England's county regiments, the 45th Regiment of Foot was granted the title Sherwood Foresters in 1866 although the regimental records show that the name had an even earlier provenance. Serving in the army of Henry V at Agincourt in 1415 was a group of Nottinghamshire archers who fought under the name of 'Sherwood Foresters', carrying a banner that the Warwickshire-born poet Michael Drayton described in his long poem *The Battaile of Agincourt* (1627):

> Olde Nottingham, an Archer clad in greene,
> Under a Tree with his drawne Bowe that stood,
> Which in a checkquer'd Flagge farre off was seene:
> It was the Picture of olde Robin Hood.

The 45th's origins can be traced back to 1741 when it enjoyed close links with the county of Nottinghamshire; but when the modern regiment known as The Sherwood Foresters came into being in 1881 as the result of amalgamating with the 95th Foot its county title was that of neighbouring Derbyshire and the depot was situated at Normanton Barracks in Derby. The buildings were

A battalion of The Sherwood Foresters (Nottinghamshire and Derbyshire Regiment) advance along the Amiens–St. Quentin Road from Foucancourt in March 1917. During the conflict the Regiment expanded to 33 battalions, of which 20 served overseas.

demolished in 1981 and the land is now known as the Foresters' Leisure Park; nearby, the old regimental garrison church of St Giles is still extant. Not until 1902 was Nottinghamshire added to the regiment's title.

In recognition of that county connection, the regiment's original 3rd Battalion was called The Robin Hood Rifles and that name lived on after the founding of the Territorial Force in 1908 when it became the 7th (Robin Hood) Battalion. Under that title it mobilised in Nottingham in August 1914 and formed part of 139th Forester Brigade, one of the first Territorial brigades to see active service in France. By the end of the following year the Robin Hoods had been involved in heavy fighting at the Hohenzollern Redoubt during the Battle of Loos, where Captain C. G. Vickers, a Nottingham man, was awarded the Victoria Cross for fending off a German attack even though he realised that in so doing he was in danger of cutting off his own means of escape. Vickers survived and after the war went on to enjoy a successful career as a prominent lawyer and social scientist. In his autobiography he described in starkly realistic terms his reasons for joining up: 'In August Germany invaded Belgium, we had a treaty with Belgium, so we all stopped what we were doing and went off to war. It was as simple as that.'

Very different in his approach was another officer, Albert Ball, from Lenton in Nottingham, who joined The Robin Hood Battalion at the outbreak of war and after taking private flying lessons transferred to the Royal Flying Corps (RFC). He proved to be a naturally ruthless and skilful pilot and after joining his squadron on the Western Front he became a recognised 'ace' who enjoyed considerable fame in the British press. By the time of his death in May 1917 he was credited with forty-four victories, the fourth highest score in the history of the RFC. Ball was also highly decorated; he won the Victoria Cross posthumously, three Distinguished Service Orders and the Military Cross. He is commemorated by a memorial statue in the grounds of Nottingham Castle and by the creation of the Albert Ball Homes in his native Lenton to house the families of local servicemen killed in action.

Other notable Forester battalions in the First World War included the 16th (Chatsworth Rifles) and 17th (Welbeck Rangers), both of which experienced hard fighting during the Battle of the Somme in 1916. Both represented distinctive communities: the Chatsworth Rifles were raised by the Duke of Devonshire and named after Chatsworth House, his family seat on the River Derwent in the Peak District, while the Welbeck Rangers owed their existence to the exertions of the Mayor of Nottingham and were named after the Welbeck estate, part of which sits in Sherwood Forest. It is still a thriving concern and at its heart is historic Welbeck Abbey, seat of the Duke of Portland. In 1917 Corporal Ernest Egerton of The Chatsworth Rifles was awarded the Victoria Cross for demonstrating exceptional bravery during the Third Battle of Ypres when in quick succession he shot dead three German soldiers and took the surrender of twenty-nine more. Afterwards Egerton explained that he had just received news of his soldier brother's death and that he was 'longing to get into action and pay back a debt'. During the First World War The Sherwood Foresters lost 11,409 soldiers killed in action and their sacrifice is commemorated in the city's war memorial in Trent Park, which was unveiled on Armistice Day 1927.

Derbyshire's contribution to the regiment is no less significant. When the 95th was formed in 1823 it was the sixth regiment to be given that number, which had previously been held by The Rifle Brigade. Two years later it was given the additional title of Derbyshire Regiment, thereby beginning a connection with the county which has lasted throughout its existence. During those fifty-eight years the regiment attracted a number of officers who enjoyed successful careers in the British Army. Among the most prominent was Horace Smith-Dorrien, who joined the 95th after leaving Sandhurst and narrowly missed being awarded the Victoria Cross during the Zulu War of 1879. Only because the nomination was passed through the wrong channels did he not get the award. Nothing daunted, Smith-Dorrien rose steadily up the promotion ladder, seeing service in the Sudan and South Africa where he caught the eye of Lord Kitchener. At the outbreak of the First World War he commanded II Corps in the British Expeditionary Force and led them with great skill during the rearguard action at Le Cateau at the end of August 1914. Despite that success he was sacked nine months later with the immortal words: ''Orace, you're for 'ome!' (The speaker was General Sir William Robertson, Chief of the Imperial General Staff, who had started his career in the ranks and allegedly dropped his aitches.)

The 95th's finest hour came during the Crimean War where they played a conspicuous part in all the major land battles. At the Battle of the Alma the regiment suffered heavy losses and it was left to Private James Keenan to carry the Regimental Colour in the final stages of the battle. So fierce was the fighting that, according to

Men of a battalion of The Sherwood Foresters (Nottinghamshire and Derbyshire Regiment) make the best of the conditions in the trenches on the Western Front.

a letter written by Private Bloomfield, some Russian soldiers 'even got up trees so that they could get a good shot at us, but we saw them and brought them off their perch. Some of these when falling from the trees ... would catch their feet or clothes in some part of the tree and hang there for hours.' In the subsequent Battle of Inkerman, there were not enough officers to carry the Colours and they were brought on to the field by two non-commissioned officers – the Queens Colour, carried by Sergeant William McIntyre, and the Regimental Colour, carried by Sergeant John Gooding. So heavy were the casualties that only a hundred effectives remained at the end of the fighting and it was said of the regiment:

'There may be few of the 95th left, but those are as hard as nails.' This led to the 95th being nicknamed 'The Nails'. Four years later, following service during the Indian Mutiny, the 95th began the tradition of having a ram as a regimental mascot. Always known as 'Private Derby', the creature is on the strength of the regiment and it has become the tradition for the Duke of Devonshire to select a Swaledale ram from his Chatsworth Park flock and present it to the regiment and its successors.

Almost a hundred years after its creation, in 1970 The Sherwood Foresters lost its separate existence when it amalgamated with The Worcestershire Regiment (29th/36th) to form The Worcestershire and Sherwood Foresters. In August 2007 it became the 2nd Battalion, The Mercian Regiment.

---

## Battle Honours

### Pre-1914

*Carried on the Regimental Colour*
Louisburg, Rolica, Vimiera, Talavera, Busaco, Fuentes D'Onoro, Ciudad Rodrigo, Badajoz, Salamanca, Vittoria, Pyrenees, Nivelle, Orthes, Toulouse, Peninsula, Ava, Alma, Inkerman, Sevastopol, Central India, South Africa 1846–47, Egypt, 1882, Tirah, South Africa 1899–1902

### First World War (33 battalions)

*Those in bold carried on the Queen's Colour*
**Aisne 1914, 18,** Armentieres 1914, **Neuve Chapelle,** Aubers, Hooge 1915, **Loos, Somme 1916, 18,** Albert 1916, 18,

Bazentin, Delville Wood, Pozieres, Ginchy, Flers-Courcelette,
Morval, Thiepval, Le Transloy, Ancre Heights, Ancre 1916,
Arras 1917, 18, Vimy 1917, Scarpe 1917, 18, Messines 1917,
**Ypres 1917, 18,** Pilckem, Langemarck 1917, Menin Road,
Polygon Wood, Broodseinde, Poelcappelle, Passchendaele,
**Cambrai 1917, 18,** St Quentin, Bapaume 1917, Rosieres,
Villers Brettaneux, Lys, Bailleul, Kemmel, Scherpenberg,
Amiens, Drocourt-Queant, Hindenburg Line, Epehy, Canal du
Nord, **St Quentin Canal,** Beaurevoir, Courtrai, Selle, Sambre,
**France and Flanders 1914–18,** Piavé, **Italy 1917–18,** Suvla,
Landing at Suvla, Scimitar Hill, **Gallipoli 1915,** Egypt 1916

## Second World War

*Those in bold carried on the Queen's Colour*
**Norway 1940,** St Omer-La Bassee, Ypres-Comines Canal,
Dunkirk 1940, North-West Europe 1940, **Gazala, El Alamein,**
Djebel Guerba, Tamera, Medejez Plain, **Tunis,** North Africa
1942–43, **Salerno,** Volturno Crossing, Monte Camino, **Anzio,**
**Campoleone,** Advance to Tiber, **Gothic Line, Coriano,** Cosina
Canal Crossing, Monte Ceco, Italy 1943–45, **Singapore**
**Island,** Malaya 1942

## Recipients of the Victoria Cross

Private Bernard McQuirt, 95th Regiment, Indian
    Mutiny, 1858
Lieutenant (later Captain) Henry Singleton Pennell,
    2nd Battalion, Tirah Campaign, 1897
Private (later Corporal) William Bees, 1st Battalion, Second
    Boer War, 1901
Corporal (later Captain) Harry Churchill Beet, 1st Battalion,
    Second Boer War, 1901
Private Jacob Rivers, 1st Battalion, First World War, 1915
Corporal James Upton, 1st Battalion, First World War, 1915

Captain (Acting Lieutenant Colonel) Bernard William Vann,
1/6th Battalion, First World War, 1918

Second Lieutenant (Temporary Captain, later Colonel) Charles
Geoffrey Vickers, 7th Battalion, First World War, 1915

Corporal (later Sergeant) Ernest Albert Egerton,
16th Battalion, First World War, 1917

Acting Corporal (later Sergeant) Fred Greaves, 9th Battalion,
First World War, 1917

Captain (Temporary Lieutenant Colonel, later Major General)
Charles Edward Hudson, 2nd Battalion, First World
War, 1918

Sergeant William Henry Johnson, 1/5th Battalion, First World
War, 1918

# The Loyal Regiment (North Lancashire)

## 47th and 81st

With the prominent red rose in its cap badge and its depot in Preston, The Loyals were the epitome of a Lancashire regiment, and to underline that connection its regimental district included the towns of Bolton, Chorley, Farnworth and Hindley. But for all that it spent much of its life as the county regiment of north Lancashire it owed its main title to the junior 81st Regiment which was raised in 1793 as the Loyal Lincoln Volunteers and which later became the 81st (Loyal Lincoln Volunteers) Foot. In 1881 it amalgamated with the much older 47th (Lancashire) Foot to form The Loyal Regiment (North Lancashire), which also included the part-time 3rd Duke of Lancaster's Own Royal Lancashire Militia and the 11th and 14th Lancashire Rifle Volunteer Corps.

Known as 'The Lancashire Lads' The Loyals were one of seven infantry regiments which recruited inside the county and from the very beginning the regimental depot was at Fulwood Barracks in Preston; this is still standing today and is home to the Lancashire Infantry Museum. Built in the 1830s in the wake of the Chartist riots, Fulwood Barracks is considered to be one of the finest surviving examples of early Victorian military architecture. It is also thought to be the most haunted. In 1861 a young

243

Men of 1st Battalion The Loyal Regiment (North Lancashire), board the troopship *Nevasa* at Penang following service in Malaya, 1960.

soldier named Patrick McCaffery serving in the 32nd (Cornwall Light Infantry) Regiment deliberately shot two officers in cold blood as they were crossing the square outside the East Wing (since demolished). Both men were wounded but died a day later and McCaffery was sent to Liverpool for trial. He was found guilty and sentenced to be hanged at the beginning of January 1862. A crowd of 30,000 witnessed the execution and according to the *Liverpool Mercury* they were much affected by the fate of the twenty-year-old soldier from County Kildare: 'When the bolt was drawn, shrieks burst from many of the spectators, and several of the females left the ground weeping and wringing their hands, apparently suffering intense agony at the spectacle they had witnessed.' Within days the event had been commemorated in a penny ballad which still enjoys wide currency, thanks largely to the poignancy of the story:

> So come all you officers take advice from me
> And go treat your men with some decency
> For it's only lies and a tyranny
> That have made a martyr of McCaffery.

To this day the ghost of Patrick McCaffery is supposed to haunt the Officers' Mess in the old Block 57 while another unquiet spirit has been sensed or seen in the Garrison Chapel of St Alban, which is still in use by the British Army.

Unlike most English line infantry regiments, the 47th was raised in Scotland, in this case in 1741 by Sir John Mordaunt, a young colonel and a Whig supporter who had served with the Duke of Cumberland in Flanders and would continue to serve under him in the campaign against the Jacobite rebels in 1745 and 1746. Ten years after its foundation it was numbered 47th and was sent to Canada to join the forces led by Major General James Wolfe in his campaign to drive the French from the eastern seaboard. It was present at the siege of Louisburg in 1758 when it was given the nickname of 'Wolfe's Own' for its part in the amphibious operations which led to the capture of the huge fortress. Before embarking for Canada a sergeant in the 47th's Grenadier Company called Ned Botwood composed 'Hot Stuff', a ballad that quickly became hugely popular throughout the army. Botwood was killed in action at an inconsequential skirmish at Montmorency shortly before the decisive battle at the Plains of Abraham which led to the capture of Quebec in 1759, but the stirring words of his ballad lived on:

> Come, each death-doing dog that dares venture his
>     neck,
> Come, follow the hero that goes to Quebec;
> Jump aboard of the transports, and loose every sail,
> Pay your debts at the tavern by giving leg-bail
>     [running away];
> And ye that love fighting shall soon have enough;
> Wolfe commands us, my boys, we shall give them
>     Hot Stuff.

The 47th went on to serve with distinction in North America and in the wars against Revolutionary France, where they took part in the siege of San Sebastian in 1813. Emerging from the battle the regiment had lost most of its officers and was left under the command of a wounded subaltern. During the Crimean War the regiment was commanded by Lieutenant Colonel Hely who was badly wounded and unhorsed during the Battle of Inkerman. He would have fallen into Russian hands but for the courage and determination of Private John McDermond, a Scot from Glasgow, who rescued him and was later awarded the Victoria Cross for his actions, the only one to be made to a soldier of the 47th. A painting depicting his bravery hangs in Fulwood Barracks.

By way of contrast, the 81st Regiment was raised in Lincolnshire on the other side of England where most of its first soldiers had served originally as Volunteers. It came into being at the end of the nineteenth century as the Loyal Lincoln Volunteers and was the only regiment in the British Army to retain the word 'loyal' in its title during its 200-year existence. The regiment won battle honours at Maida, Corunna and the Peninsula and also at Ali Masjid during the Second Afghan War of 1878–80 when it was part of the Peshawar Valley Field Force, under the command of Lieutenant General Sir Sam Browne VC. Following the amalgamation, 1st Loyals (as the 47th had become) served in the Boer War under the command of Lieutenant Colonel Robert Kekewich who also found himself in charge of the garrison at Kimberley during its lengthy siege. Described as an unassuming man with strong nerves, Kekewich soon found himself at loggerheads with the influential imperialist businessman and politician Cecil Rhodes and ended the war leading his Loyals as mounted infantry.

After the outbreak of the First World War, The Loyals raised twenty-one battalions for service on the main battlefronts. Among them was the 7th Battalion which

Bren gun carriers of 2nd Battalion The Loyal Regiment (North Lancashire) training in Singapore in 1941. Following the Japanese attack the following year and the collapse of the garrison, they became prisoners of war of the Japanese.

formed a 'Preston Businessmen and Clerks' Company' (D Company) for service on the Western Front. It was later joined by three other similar companies from Blackpool, Kirkham and Chorley and saw action on the Somme where the battalion's casualties were ten officers and 213 other ranks, killed, wounded or missing. Their memorial is mounted within Preston railway station, perhaps the last sight of their home county many of the young soldiers had before they departed for the front. It was unveiled in 2012 and is a companion piece to the cenotaph designed by Sir Giles Gilbert Scott, which was unveiled in June 1926 to commemorate Preston's 1,956 war dead. It stands on a spot overlooking the Market Place where the 'Preston Pals' first paraded in late summer 1914. The names of the dead are listed on the handsome marble Roll of Honour in the nearby Harris Museum, Art Gallery and Library. In 1970 The Loyals amalgamated with The Lancashire Regiment (Prince of Wales's Volunteers) to form The Queen's Lancashire Regiment and in turn this became part of The Duke of Lancaster's Regiment which continues to have its headquarters at Fulwood Barracks in Preston.

---

## Battle Honours

### Pre-1914

*Carried on the Regimental Colour*
Maida, Corunna, Tarifa, Vittoria, San Sebastian, Nive,
Peninsula, Ava, Alma; Inkermann Sevastopol, Ali Masjid,
Afghanistan 1878–9, Defence of Kimberley, South Africa
1899–1902; Mediterranean 1900–01

## First World War (21 battalions)

*Those in bold carried on the Queen's Colour*
**Mons,** Retreat from Mons, Marne 1914, 18, **Aisne 1914,
1918, Ypres 1914, 17, 18,** Langemarck 1914, Gheluvelt,
Nonne Bosschen, Givenchy 1914, Aubers, Festubert 1915,
Loos, **Somme 1916, 18,** Albert 1916, Bazentin, Pozieres,
Guillemont, Ginchy, Flers-Courcelette, Morval, Ancre Heights,
Ancre 1916, Arras 1917, 18, Scarpe 1917, Arleux, Messines
1917, Pilckem, Menin Road, Polygon Wood, Poelcapelle,
Passchendaele, Cambrai 1917, 18, St Quentin, Bapaume 1918,
**Lys,** Estaires, Bailleul, Kemmel, Béthune, Scherpenberg,
Soissonnais-Ourcq, Drocourt-Quéant, **Hindenburg Line,**
Epéhy, Canal du Nord, St Quentin Canal, Courtrai, Selle,
Sambre, France and Flanders 1914–18, Doiran 1917,
Macedonia 1917, **Suvla,** Sari Bair, Gallipoli 1915,
Egypt 1916, **Gaza,** Nebi Samwil, Jerusalem, Jaffa, Tell Asur,
Palestine 1917–18, Tigris 1916, Kut al Amara 1917, **Baghdad,**
Mesopotamia 1916–18, **Kilimanjaro,** East Africa 1914–16

## Second World War

*Those in bold carried on the Queen's Colour*
**Dunkirk 1940,** North-West Europe 1940, Banana Island,
**Djebel Kess Kiss,** Mediez Plain, **Gueriat el Atach Ridge,** Djebel
Bou Aoukaz 1943, Gab Gab Gap, **North Africa 1943, Anzio,**
Rome, **Fiesole,** Gothic Line, Monte Gamberaldi, Monte Ceco,
**Monte Grande, Italy 1944–45, Johore,** Batu Pahat, **Singapore
Island,** Malaya 1941–42

## Recipients of the Victoria Cross

Private John McDermond, 47th Regiment, Crimea, 1854
Private (later Sergeant) Henry Edward Kenny, 1st Battalion,
  First World War, 1915

Lieutenant Thomas Orde Lawder Wilkinson, 7th Battalion,
First World War, 1916

Lieutenant Richard Basil Brandram Jones, 8th Battalion,
First World War, 1916

Lieutenant Willward Alexander Sandys-Clarke, 1st Battalion,
Second World War, 1943

# The Middlesex Regiment
# (Duke of Cambridge's Own)

## 57th and 77th

The Middlesex Regiment gained an enviable nickname when one of its antecedents, the 57th (West Middlesex) Foot, went into battle at Albuera in Spain on 16 May 1811 during the Peninsula campaign against Napoleonic France. In the course of a determined French attack on the British lines its commanding officer, Lieutenant Colonel William Inglis, was shot from his horse and lay badly wounded in front of his men. Despite the severity of his injuries he refused to be carried to the rear and instead continued to shout encouragement to his beleaguered men, exhorting them with words that were to become famous: 'Die hard, the 57th, die hard!' The casualties in the 57th were 422 out of the 570 men in the ranks and 20 out of the 30 officers but the line held and, astonishingly, Inglis survived his wounds. As a result the regiment was nicknamed 'The Die-Hards'.

Raised in 1741, the 57th had a close association with the county of Middlesex, which supplied it with most of its recruits, and throughout its existence the regiment maintained its depot and headquarters in Mill Hill, now part of the London Borough of Barnet. In 1909 new barracks named after Colonel Inglis were built on ground at Brittacy Farm and were occupied by the

Officers and men of 1st Battalion The Middlesex Regiment on the dockside in Hong Kong following their operational service in Korea, August 1951. Together with the Argyll and Sutherland Highlanders the regiment had been the first British forces to take part in the war.

regiment until 1962. For a time the buildings were used by the army's postal services and in 1988 the Provisional IRA attacked the barracks, killing one soldier in a bomb blast. Over the years most of the land was sold off for private housing development and all that remains of the military presence is Mill Hill East Station, which was expanded in 1941 to cater for the barracks in wartime.

In 1881 the 57th was amalgamated with the 77th (East Middlesex) Foot, the Duke of Cambridge's Own, to form The Middlesex Regiment with two (later four) Regular battalions, two Militia battalions and four Volunteer battalions composed of part-time soldiers from the local community. In 1908, with the formation of the Territorial Force (later Territorial Army), the volunteer battalions became the 7th, 8th, 9th and 10th Battalions. The regimental Colonel-in-Chief was Prince George, Duke of Cambridge, the army's commander-in-chief and cousin of Queen Victoria, who had a reputation as a traditionalist. He once offered a stinging rebuke to a subordinate with intellectual pretensions: 'Brains? I don't believe in brains! You haven't any, I know, sir!'

Both the 57th and the 77th had seen service all over the Empire and both were involved in the Crimean War of 1854–56 where three soldiers were awarded the newly introduced Victoria Cross for conspicuous bravery – Sergeant John Park of the 77th, during the battles of the Alma and Inkerman, Sergeant George Gardiner of the 57th and Private Alexander Wright of the 77th, both during the siege of Sevastopol. However, it was during the First World War that the men of Middlesex really showed their mettle.

The regiment was one of five in the British Army that had four Regular battalions before the outbreak of the conflict in August 1914; it also had two Special Reserve battalions (5th and 6th) and four Territorial battalions, 7th to 10th. During the course of the war another thirty-nine battalions were formed, making the regiment the second largest in the army along with The King's (Liverpool), though not all battalions survived to the end of the war. Losses amounted to 12,720, eighty-one battle honours were awarded to the regiment and five soldiers were awarded the Victoria Cross. The Middlesex were in action right from the outset of the fighting: the first soldier of the British Expeditionary Force to be killed in France was Lance Corporal John Parr from North Finchley who served with 4th Middlesex and was killed in action on 21 August 1914. By unhappy coincidence the first British officer to be killed in France served in the same battalion: Major W. H. Abell of Norton Hall, Worcestershire, was killed at Mons two days later. The regiment served on all battlefronts, including an intervention by the 25th Middlesex in support of anti-Bolshevik forces in Murmansk in 1919. This involved a lengthy journey across Siberia which the battalion met with customary phlegm, their commanding officer noting: 'One and all behaved like Englishmen – the highest eulogy that can be passed upon the conduct of men.'

Perhaps the best known wartime battalion was the 17th Middlesex, which was composed almost entirely of professional footballers from the regimental area. The entire Clapton Orient (later Leyton Orient) football team and ground staff joined up early in the war, stating clearly that they wanted to be part of the 17th 'Footballers'

Amongst this group of officers in Vladivostok in 1919 are men of the 25th Battalion The Middlesex Regiment. They were deployed at the end of the First World War as part of the a multi-national Allied Intervention Force supporting the anti-Bolshevik White army in the Russian Civil War.

Battalion' and by early 1915 there were 122 professional footballers in its ranks. Among them was Captain Walter Tull, a player with Northampton Town FC who also had the distinction of being the army's first black officer of the war. The wartime services of those young footballers were recognised on Saturday 30 April 1921 when the Prince of Wales, later King Edward VIII, visited Millfields Road Stadium to watch Clapton Orient play Notts County. The home team won 3-0. This was the first time a member of the British Royal Family had attended a Football League match, the royal visit having been arranged to show gratitude for Clapton Orient's patriotic example. Although the stadium has long since been demolished to make way for housing, a plaque erected on the site commemorates this historic event. No less singular in its approach was the regiment's 16th Battalion, which was designated a 'Public Schools Battalion' and originally intended to be reserved for young men who had been privately educated at school or university. Towards the end of the war, though, very few soldiers in that battalion had any connection with Middlesex or, indeed, the country's public schools.

At the beginning of the Second World War 1st Middlesex Regiment was based in Hong Kong and, in common with the rest of the garrison, went into Japanese captivity following the capitulation of the Crown colony at the end of 1941. However, the regiment played a valuable role throughout the war by supplying specialist machine-gun battalions to several infantry divisions in the fighting in Europe. For 1st/7th Middlesex this was something of a baptism of fire as they were posted to the 51st Highland Division whose commander, Major

General Douglas Wimberley, had made it clear that he wanted only Highland, or at the very least Lowland, Scots serving under his command. Equipped with carrier-borne medium Vickers machine guns, the four companies represented a cross section of the county of Middlesex – Highgate, Enfield, Hornsey and Tottenham – and their arrival in a division composed of Highland regiments could have been awkward. However, shortly after arriving in the north of Scotland 'the Cockneys made themselves appreciated and became friends for life with the Highlanders, civilian and military alike'.

That link between The Middlesex Regiment and the Scots was reinforced in 1950 when 1st Middlesex Regiment and 1st Argyll and Sutherland Highlanders formed a weakened infantry brigade which was rushed to South Korea to support US forces following the outbreak of war with North Korea. As the novelist Eric Linklater put it in the Official History of the conflict, both regiments had to draw deeply on their history and traditions: 'In the months to come both the Middlesex and the Argylls – though nearly half of them were youngsters doing their national training – were to enhance the pride and reputation, not only of the Diehards and the 91st, but of all the Army.'

In 1966 the Middlesex Regiment became the 4th Battalion of the newly created Queen's Regiment, but it was disbanded in 1970 and in the years that followed the Middlesex lineage became increasingly obscure. By the time The Queen's amalgamated with The Royal Hampshire Regiment in 1992 to form The Princess of Wales's Royal Regiment, in reality the old connections with Mill Hill had long since disappeared.

# Battle Honours

## Pre-1914

*Carried on the Regimental Colour*

Mysore, Seringapatam, Peninsula, Albuhera, Ciudad Rodrigo, Badajoz, Nive, Nivelle, Pyrenees, Vittoria, Alma, Inkerman, Sevastopol, New Zealand, South Africa 1879, Relief of Ladysmith, South Africa 1900–02

## First World War (46 battalions)

*Those in bold carried on the Queen's Colour*

**Mons**, Le Cateau, Retreat from Mons, **Marne 1914**, Aisne 1914, 18, La Bassée 1914, Messines 1914, 17, 18, Armentières 1914, Neuve Chapelle, **Ypres 1915, 17, 18**, Gravenstafel, St. Julien, Frezenberg, Bellewaarde, Aubers, Hooge 1915, Loos, Somme 1916, 18, **Albert 1916, 18, Bazentin**, Delville Wood, Pozières, Ginchy, Flers-Courcelette, Morval, Thiepval, Le Transloy, Ancre Heights, Ancre 1916, 18, Bapaume 1917, 18, Arras 1917, 18, Vimy 1917, Scarpe 1917, 18, Arleux, Pilckem, Langemarck 1917, Menin Road, Polygon Wood, Broodseinde, Poelcappelle, Passchendaele, **Cambrai 1917, 18**, St. Quentin, Rosières, Avre, Villers Bretonneux, Lys, Estaires, Hazebrouck, Bailleul, Kemmel, Scherpenberg, **Hindenburg Line**, Canal du Nord, St. Quentin Canal, Courtrai, Selle, Valenciennes, Sambre, France and Flanders 1914–18, Italy 1917–18, Struma, Doiran 1918, Macedonia 1915–18, **Suvla**, Landing at Suvla, Scimitar Hill, Gallipoli 1915, Rumani, Egypt 1915–17, Gaza, **Jerusalem**, Jericho, Jordan, Tell 'Asur, Palestine 1917–18, **Mesopotamia 1917–18**, Murman 1919, Dukhovskaya, Siberia 1918–19

The Middlesex Regiment (Duke of Cambridge's Own)

## Second World War

*Those in bold carried on the Queen's Colour*
Dyle, Defence of Escaut, Ypres-Comines Canal, **Dunkirk 1940, Normandy Landing,** Cambes, Breville, Odon, Caen, Orne, Hill 112, Bourguébus Ridge, Troarn, **Mont Pincon,** Falaise, Seine 1944, Nederrijn, Le Havre, Lower Maas, Venraij, Meijel, Geilenkirchen, Venlo Pocket, Rhineland, Reichswald, Goch, **Rhine,** Lingen, Brinkum, Bremen, North-West Europe 1940, 44–45, **El Alamein,** Advance on Tripoli, Mareth, **Akarit,** Djebel Roumana, North Africa 1942–43, Francofonte, Sferro, Sferro Hills, **Sicily 1943, Anzio,** Carroceto, Gothic Line, Monte Grande, Italy 1944–45, **Hong Kong,** South-East Asia 1941

## Post-1945 (1st Battalion)

*Carried on the Regimental Colour*
**Naktong Bridgehead,** Chongju, Chongchon II Chuam-Ni, Kapyong-chon, Kapyong, **Korea 1950–51**

## Recipients of the Victoria Cross

Sergeant John Park, 77th Regiment, Crimean War, 1854
Colour Sergeant George Gardiner, 57th Regiment, Crimean War, 1855
Private Charles McCorrie, 57th Regiment, Crimean War, 1855
Private Alexander Wright 77th Regiment, Crimean War, 1855
Ensign John Thornton Down, 57th Regiment, Maori War, 1860
Drummer Dudley Stagpoole, 57th Regiment, Maori War, 1860
2nd Lieutenant Rupert Price Hallowes, 4th Battalion, First World War, 1915
Private (later Corporal) Frederick Jeremiah Edwards, 12th Battalion, First World War, 1916

Private (later Sergeant) Robert Edward Ryder, 12th Battalion,
First World War, 1916
Captain Allastair McReady-Diarmid, 17th Battalion,
First World War, 1917
Captain (later Brigadier) Alfred Maurice Toye, 2nd Battalion,
First World War, 1918

# The York and Lancaster Regiment

## 65th and 84th

This is the regiment whose original county title was never used because no one knew what it was supposed to represent. When the 65th Foot and the 84th Foot were selected for amalgamation in 1881, the title proposed for the new regiment was The Hallamshire Regiment. It was intended to recognise the fact that the regiment's recruiting area would include a part of South Yorkshire known as Hallamshire that embraces modern Sheffield, Ecclesfield and Bradfield. However, the proposal was highly un-popular as the name Hallamshire was unfamiliar and considered archaic, even though it was eventually used by the regiment's 4th Territorial Battalion, previously the Hallamshire Volunteer Rifle Corps. To resolve the issue a vote was taken among the officers who chose York and Lancaster in recognition of the fact that it was the territorial title of the 84th Foot, which enjoyed historic links with both the city of York and the north Lancashire garrison town of Preston, home to its 2nd Battalion in 1808. However, the regiment's title refers not to the modern counties of Lancashire and Yorkshire but to the ancient Duchies of Lancaster and York and was a reminder of the Wars of the Roses and the historical rivalry between the houses of York and Lancaster. This

Recruitment poster for The York and Lancaster Regiment published by Gale and Polden Limited in 1946.

was symbolised in the use of the Tudor rose in the regiment's cap badge, marrying the white rose of York and the red of Lancaster. It sat above a Royal Bengal tiger which was awarded in 1823 and gives rise to the badge's colloquial nickname 'the cat and cabbage.'

When the boundaries between the modern counties were being drawn in the mid-nineteenth century a large part of the Duchy of Lancaster was incorporated within the West Riding of Yorkshire. Basically, the regiment always considered itself to be affiliated to Yorkshire with its main recruiting area in the south of the county incorporating the major towns of Barnsley, Sheffield and Rotherham. On its formation in 1881 that relationship was cemented with the construction of the new regiment's brick-built depot which was situated in Pontefract and it still stands in Wakefield Road. It closed in 1963 and is now a business centre. The York and Lancs (also known locally as the Young and Lovelies) was a relatively short-lived regiment. In 1968 it agreed that, instead of amalgamating with another Yorkshire regiment and losing its separate identity, it would choose disbandment. The final parade was held in Sheffield on 14 December 1968 and the Regimental Colours were laid up in the Chapel of St George in Sheffield Cathedral.

The older component of the regiment began life in 1758 when it was founded as the 2nd Battalion of the 12th Regiment of Foot, later to become The Suffolk Regiment. This was very much an emergency measure to increase the size of the army during the Seven Years War, the idea being to add a second battalion to a number of regiments which were reasonably well recruited. The scheme was so successful that within the same year the new regiment was given its own number and was retitled the 65th Regiment of Foot with its recruiting area being designated in 1782 as the North Riding of Yorkshire. It soon saw active service when it was part of a force of six infantry regiments sent to the West Indies in the following year with the objective of capturing the French 'sugar islands' of Guadeloupe, Martinique and Cuba. These were valuable acquisitions but as an early regimental historian explained, the operation placed great strains on those taking part: 'The troops, unaccustomed to the climate, suffered greatly from fevers, from the flux, the scurvy from the use of salt provisions and from an accidental evil, the smallpox, which broke out amongst the transports.'

It was a difficult birth for the young regiment but it survived the dreadful hardships and was able to return home with the battle honour 'Guadeloupe 1759', to be stationed in Ireland, where it remained until 1768. Later in the century the 65th served in North America and the Caribbean and its travels continued during the Napoleonic Wars when it was stationed in Mauritius and India. Perhaps its most unusual period of service within the Empire came when it was based in Australia and New Zealand between 1845 and 1865. In the latter country the regiment took part in the Land Wars between the colonists and the native Maoris who provided the regiment with its nickname 'Hickety Pip' from their pronunciation of the number 65th.

The records also show that, despite being on opposite sides, there was a good deal of mutual respect: when pickets from the 65th went into the bush at night they would identify themselves to the Maori warriors and ask them if there would be fighting that night. If the reply was 'Not tonight – too wet and cold; we'd better get some sleep. Good night, Hickety Pip' both sides would honour the agreement. If there was to be an attack, they would be given a warning and would be expected to fight like any other regiment. While taking part in the Waikato Campaign of 1863–65 two soldiers were awarded the Victoria Cross – Colour Sergeant Edward McKenna from Leeds and Lance Corporal John Ryan from County Tipperary, both of whom demonstrated supreme gallantry under fire after their officers had been killed. McKenna stayed in the country after the 65th returned to England and joined the New Zealand Railways. Sadly, a year later, Ryan died while attempting to save a drunken soldier from drowning in the Waikato River. His medal is on display in the York and Lancaster Museum at Clifton Park in Rotherham.

By contrast the 84th Regiment of Foot had a much less settled beginning. It was formed in 1759 for service in India, its first Colonel being Eyre Coote, who had already seen meritorious service in India, fighting under Robert Clive at the Battle of Plassey. Despite his later fame as one of the creators of British India, Coote, born in Kilmallock in County Limerick, had experienced an indifferent start to his military career. Commissioned into Blakeney's Regiment of Foot (later the 27th), he lost his nerve and ran away while in charge of the Colour Party before the Battle of Falkirk during the Jacobite uprising of 1745–46. Coote was court-martialled for cowardice but survived to fight another day in India and the 84th fought with great credit in the First Mysore War. Even so it was disbanded in 1763 and when it was raised once again, this time by Colonel Allan Maclean in 1775, it was given the title The

Royal Highland Emigrants and earmarked for service in Canada. The men wore Highland dress with Black Watch tartan and among those who served in the regiment was Allan Macdonald of Kingsburgh, the husband of Flora MacDonald, the saviour of Bonnie Prince Charlie when he was on the run in the Highlands after Culloden. Again it was a short-lived existence, being disbanded and re-raised in its final form in 1793 for service in the war against Revolutionary France. In 1809 it was given the new title 84th (York and Lancaster) Foot.

The new regiment won its spurs during the Indian Mutiny where it came under the command of Lieutenant General Sir James Outram, an experienced soldier known throughout the army as the 'Bayard of India' on account of his well-known courtesy and knightly virtues. When the 84th left India in 1859 he was moved to say of its service: 'A private letter is hardly a proper medium for giving expression to the strong feelings I bear to the glorious old 84th, but the feelings I do bear it are very strong, and every officer, non-commissioned officer and private of the Corps is, and ever shall be, my comrade and my friend!' During the fighting six soldiers were awarded the Victoria Cross.

---

## Battle Honours

### Pre-1914

*Carried on the Regimental Colour*
Guadeloupe 1759, Martinique 1794, Arabia, Nive, Peninsula, India, Lucknow, New Zealand, Tel-el-Kebir, Egypt 1882–84, Relief of Ladysmith, South Africa 1899–1902

## First World War (22 battalions)

*Those in bold carried on the Queen's Colour*
Aisne 1914, Armentières 1914, **Ypres 1915, 17, 18,**
Gravenstafel, St. Julien, Frezenberg, Bellewaarde, Hooge 1915,
Loos, **Somme 1916, 18,** Albert 1916, Pozières, Flers-
Courcelette, Morval, Thiepval, Le Transloy, Ancre Heights,
Ancre 1916, Arras 1917, 18, Scarpe 1917, 18, Arleux, Oppy,
**Messines 1917, 18,** Langemarck 1917, Menin Road, Polygon
Wood, Broodseinde, Poelcappelle, **Passchendaele, Cambrai
1917, 18,** St. Quentin, Bapaume 1918, **Lys,** Hazebrouck,
Bailleul, Kemmel, Scherpenberg, Marne 1918, Tardenois,
Drocourt-Quéant, Hindenburg Line, Havrincourt, Épéhy,
Canal du Nord, **Selle,** Valenciennes, Sambre, France and
Flanders 1914–18, **Piave,** Vittorio Veneto, Italy 1917–18,
Struma, Doiran 1917, **Macedonia 1915–18,** Suvla, Landing at
Suvla, Scimitar Hill, **Gallipoli 1915,** Egypt 1916

## Second World War

*Those in bold carried on the Queen's Colour*
Norway 1940, Odon, **Fontenay Le Pesnil,** Caen, La Vie Crossing,
La Touques Crossing, Forêt de Bretonne, Le Havre, **Antwerp-
Turnhout Canal,** Scheldt, Lower Maas, Arnhem 1945, North-
West Europe 1940, 44–45, **Tobruk 1941,** Tobruk Sortie 1941,
**Mine de Sedjenane,** Djebel Kournine, North Africa 1941, 43,
Landing in Sicily, Simeto Bridgehead, Pursuit to Messina, **Sicily
1943, Salerno,** Vietri Pass, Capture of Naples, Cava di Terreni,
Volturno Crossing, Monte Camino, Calabritto, Colle Cedro,
Garigliano Crossing, **Minturno,** Monte Tuga, Anzio, Advance to
Tiber, Gothic Line, Coriano, San Clemente, Gemmano Ridge,
Carpineta, Lamone Crossing, Defence of Lamone Bridgehead,
Rimini Line, San Marino, Italy 1943-45, Crete, Heraklion,
Middle East 1941, **North Arakan,** Maungdaw, Rangoon Road,
Toungoo, Arakan Beaches, **Chindits 1944,** Burma 1943–45

## Recipients of the Victoria Cross

Lance Corporal (later Lieutenant Colonel), Abraham Boulger, 84th Regiment, Indian Mutiny, 1857

Private Joel Holmes, 84th Regiment, Indian Mutiny, 1857

Sergeant Major (later Lieutenant) George Lambert, 84th Regiment, Indian Mutiny, 1857

Lance Corporal John Sinnott, 84th Regiment, Indian Mutiny, 1857

Captain (later Lieutenant Colonel) Augustus Anson, 84th Regiment, Indian Mutiny, 1857

Private (later Sergeant) Patrick Mylott, 84th Regiment, Indian Mutiny, 1857

Colour Sergeant Edward McKenna, 65th Regiment, Maori War, 1863

Lance Corporal John Ryan, 65th Regiment, Maori War, 1863

Private Samuel Harvey, 1st Battalion First World War, 1915

Private John Caffrey, 2nd Battalion First World War, 1915

Sergeant Frederick Charles Riggs, 6th Battalion, First World War, 1918

Sergeant John Brunton Daykins, 2/4th Battalion, First World War, 1918

Corporal John William Harper, 4th Hallamshire Battalion, Second World War, 1944

# The Durham Light Infantry

## 68th and 106th

From the very beginning, long before the advent of county affiliations for English infantry regiments, the 68th Regiment of Foot had an established connection with County Durham. It was founded in 1756 as the 2nd Battalion of the 23rd Foot, the regiment that later became The Royal Welch Fusiliers, but two years later it received its own identity by being redesignated the 68th Foot. Its first Colonel was John Lambton, an officer in the Coldstream Guards who inherited Harraton Hall in County Durham, which was demolished in 1797 to make way for the later Lambton Castle. In 1761 Lambton became MP for Durham City and represented the constituency in five parliaments, retiring in 1787. He also retained the colonelcy of the 68th until his death in 1794 and his grandson, known as 'Radical Jack', became the 1st Earl of Durham in 1828. It was not until 1782 that the regiment was granted the title 68th (Durham) Foot and by then most of its recruits came from within the county, many of them choosing a military career in preference to labouring in the local coal mines. A further change came in 1808 when it was made a light infantry regiment for service in the Peninsula campaign during the Napoleonic Wars, adopting the ethos and training of the newly created light infantry regiments.

Officers and men of 1st Battalion The Durham Light Infantry celebrate the birthday of HM Queen Elizabeth II while stationed in Berlin on 8 June 1963. The parade is taking place on the Maifeld in front of the Olympic Stadium.

In the early years of its existence the 68th was based in Northumberland at Hexham, Berwick-on-Tweed and Morpeth, but during the second half of the eighteenth century it mainly served abroad, in the West Indies and North America, and did not have a home station in England until after the Napoleonic Wars. During the Crimean War the regiment served in General Sir George Cathcart's 3rd Division and fought in the main battles at the Alma, Balaclava, Inkerman and the siege of Sevastopol. During the battle of Inkerman the Durhams took off their grey greatcoats and charged the Russian lines in their scarlet tunics. In honour of that brave, if foolhardy, action Inkerman Day, 5 November, was celebrated each year with senior NCOs wearing a whistle and Inkerman chain on their sashes to mark their leadership in the battle which also brought the regiment its first of eleven Victoria Crosses. It was awarded to John Byrne from Castleconnor, Kilkenny, in Ireland who had enlisted in the regiment in Coventry at seventeen. Two separate incidents distinguished him. During the Battle of Inkerman he brought in a wounded soldier under fire and during the siege of Sevastopol in the following year he defended his section of the parapet by beating off a Russian attack and killing an enemy soldier in hand-to-hand combat. Byrne reached the rank of sergeant and was discharged in 1872 but fell into bad habits and while working in Wales he shot dead a fellow labourer who had insulted the Victoria Cross. When the police came to arrest him he committed suicide by shooting himself in the mouth. For years Byrne lay buried in an unmarked grave in Newport but in 1985 a headstone was erected bearing his name and it was unveiled by General Sir Peter de la Billière who had started his military career in 1st Durham Light Infantry.

Best known as the commander of the British Forces in the Middle East during the Gulf War of 1990–91, de la Billière joined the Durhams in 1952 before transferring to the 22nd SAS Regiment, which he later commanded. Other distinguished men who served in the Durham Light Infantry were the conductor and composer Sir Malcolm Sargent, Tottenham Hotspur Football Club manager Bill Nicholson, the actor Leslie Phillips and King Vajiravudh, of Siam while he was Crown Prince.

By contrast the other constituent regiment of the Durham Light Infantry had a very different history and background. It started life in 1839 in the service of the Honourable East India Company as the 2nd Bombay (European) Regiment and was redesignated 2nd Bombay (European) Light Infantry in 1844. In that guise it took part in a short but conclusive war against Persia in 1856 and the Indian Mutiny of the following year. Following the reorganisation of British rule it became part of the British Army in 1862 as the 106th Regiment (Bombay Light Infantry). Under the Cardwell reforms of 1881 it amalgamated with the 68th to form The Durham Light Infantry, becoming its 2nd Battalion. The badge of the new regiment was a stringed bugle beneath the crown with the letters DLI and its first depot was Fenham Barracks in Newcastle, which it shared with The Northumberland Fusiliers. It took another half-century and two world wars before the Durhams moved back into their home county when Brancepeth Castle, to the south of Durham, became the regimental depot. The original castle was built in Norman times and for many years was in the possession of the Neville family until it was confiscated in 1569 following an unsuccessful plot against Queen Elizabeth I. In its time as the regimental depot the castle's grounds spawned a huge hutted army encampment. It is now in private hands.

During the First World War the Durhams raised forty-three battalions with twenty-two of them seeing active service overseas, on the Western Front, in Italy, Egypt, Salonika and India. One of their volunteer soldiers was also the first casualty of enemy action on British soil when German warships bombarded Hartlepool on 16 December 1914, killing Private Theophilus Jones, 18th Durham Light Infantry, as well as six others manning two artillery batteries at Heugh Point. A memorial plaque marks the spot. Formed at Cocken Hall near Finchale, the 18th Durhams was one of four 'pals' battalions raised by the regiment in the opening weeks of the war and comprised of men from the same communities. Most of the men in this battalion came from Durham, Darlington, Hartlepool, Middlesbrough, Stockton, Sunderland and Bishop Auckland. The other battalions were the 19th, the 20th (Wearside) and the 22nd and all four distinguished themselves on the Western Front. Together with other 'pals' battalions from the north of England the 18th battalion saw action on 1 July 1916, the first day of the Battle of the Somme, going into the attack at Serre on the northern end of the battlefield where 300 men were killed or wounded in four days of heavy fighting. Among those who went over the top at 07.30 was Lance Corporal Charles Moss, a machine-gunner with C Company who remembered bumping into a fellow soldier 'who seemed to be carrying a big piece of raw meat resting on his left arm … then I realised it was the remains of his right forearm he was carrying.' Moss's diary is held in the

Men of 11th Battalion The Durham Light Infantry being transported by light railway to take part in the Battle of Pilkem Ridge on 31 July 1917. They are seen passing Elverdinghe in Belgium.

Durham County Record Office, which houses the regimental archives.

During the Second World War the regiment maintained its proud tradition of service, raising eleven battalions to serve in North-West Europe, North Africa, Sicily, Italy and Burma. During the retreat to Dunkirk in May 1940, 2nd Lieutenant R. W. 'Dickie' Annand, 2nd Durhams, was awarded the first army Victoria Cross of the conflict when he twice attacked German positions on the River Dyle before returning to rescue his wounded batman and pushing him to safety in a wheelbarrow. The regiment's last battle honour was gained when the 1st Battalion was deployed to South Korea in September 1952 as part of UN forces deployed against North Korea and China. The regimental Korean War memorial, the statue of a bugler in combat uniform, was unveiled at the National Memorial Arboretum in Staffordshire.

In 1968 1st Durham Light Infantry became the 4th Battalion of the newly raised Light Infantry Regiment, an amalgamation of England's four existing light infantry regiments, but it was disbanded a year later. Its colours were laid up in the Durham Light Infantry Chapel in the south transept of Durham Cathedral, which was consecrated in 1922 to commemorate the regiment's 12,600 casualties in the First World War. There is also a memorial garden in the Cathedral Close.

---

## Battle Honours

### Pre-1914

*Carried on the Regimental Colour*
**Salamanca, Vittoria, Pyrenees, Orthes, Peninsula, Alma, Inkerman, Sebastopol, Reshire, Bushire, Koosh-Ab, Persia, New Zealand, Relief of Ladysmith, South Africa, 1899–1902**

### First World War (43 battalions)

*Those in bold carried on the Queen's Colour*
**Aisne 1914, 18,** Armentieres 1914, **Ypres 1915, 17, 18,** Gravestafel, St Julien, Frezenberg. Bellewaarde, **Hooge 1915, Loos, Somme 1916, 18,** Albert 1916, 18, Bazentin, Delville Wood, Pozieres, Guillemont, Flers-Courcelette, Morval, Le Transloy, Ancre Heights, **Arras 1917, 18,** Scarpe 1917, Arleux, Hill 70, **Messines 1917,** Pilckem, Langemarck, 1917, Menin Road, Polygon Wood, Broodseinde, Passchendaele, Cambrai 1917, 18, St Quentin, Rosieres, **Lys,** Estaires,

Hazebrouck, Bailleul, Kemmel, Scherpenberg, Marne 1918, Tardenoi, Bapaume 1918, Hindenburg Line, Havrincourt, Epehy, Canal du Nord, St Quentin Canal, Beaurevoir, Courtrai, Selle, **Sambre,** France and Flanders 1914–18, Piave, Vittorio Veneto, Italy 1917–18, Macedonia 1916–18, Egypt 1915–16, N.W, Frontier India 1915, 1916–17, Archangel 1918–19

## Second World War

*Those in bold carried on the Queen's Colour*
Dyle, Arras Counter-attack, St Omer-La Bassee, **Dunkirk 1940,** Villers Bocage, **Tilly sur Seulles, Defence of Rauray,** St Pierre La Vielle, **Gheel,** Roer, Ibbenburen, North-West Europe 1940, 44–45, Syria 1941, Halfaya 1941, **Tobruk 1941,** Relief of Tobruk, Gazala, Gabr el Facri, Zt el Mrasses, Mersa Matruh, Point 174, **El Alamein, Mareth,** Sedjenane I, El Kourzia, North Africa 1940–43, Landing in Sicily, Solarino, **Primosolo Bridge,** Sicily 1943, **Salerno,** Volturno Crossing, 1943, Teano, Monte Camino, Monte Tuga, Gothic Line, Gemmano Ridge, Cosina Canal Crossing, Pergola Ridge, Cesena, Sillaro Crossing, Italy 1943–45, Athens, Greece 1944–45, Cos, Middle East 1943, Malta 1942, Donbaik, **Kohima,** Mandalay, Burma 1943–45

## Post-1945 (1st Battalion)

*Carried on the Regimental Colour*
**Korea 1952–53**

## Recipients of the Victoria Cross

Private John Byrne, 68th Regiment, Crimean War, 1854
Captain Thomas de Courcy Hamilton, 68th Regiment,
  Crimean War, 1857

Sergeant John Murray, 68th Regiment, Maori War, 1864

Private Thomas Kenny, 13th Battalion, First World War, 1915

Temporary Lieutenant (later Brigadier) Colonel Roland Boys
  Bradford 9th Battalion, First World War, 1916

Private Michael Heaviside, 15th Battalion, First World
  War, 1917

2nd Lieutenant Frederick Youens, 13th Battalion, First World
  War, 1917

Captain Arthur Moore Lascelles, 14th Battalion, First World
  War, 1917

Private Thomas Young, 9th Battalion, First World War, 1918

2nd Lieutenant (later Captain) Richard Wallace Annand,
  2nd Battalion, Second World War, 1940

Private Adam Herbert Wakenshaw, 9th Battalion, Second
  World War, 1942

# The Highland Light Infantry
## (City of Glasgow Regiment)

### 71st and 74th

Always known by its initials HLI, The Highland Light
Infantry also rejoiced in its nickname 'Hell's Last Issue'.
Its proper name notwithstanding, The Highland Light
Infantry was closely associated not with the Scottish
Highlands but with Glasgow, drawing most of its recruits
from the city's heavy industrial areas where men were
tough, proud and resilient; in return the people of
Glasgow took a fierce pride in their local regiment. In
1923 that relationship was cemented by the addition of
'City of Glasgow Regiment' to the regiment's formal title.
One incident among many others in the regiment's long
history underlines the strength and endurance of that
connection.

Shortly after the outbreak of the First World War,
Glasgow City Corporation gave approval for the
formation of a volunteer infantry battalion drawn from
the city's public transport system which would serve in
the HLI. Wearing their green uniforms and marching
behind a pipe band, more than 800 motormen and
conductors of the tramways department paraded through
the city on 7 September 1914 before presenting themselves
for enlistment. Under the direction of James Dalrymple,
Glasgow's transport manager, the Coplawhill tramways

A Guard of Honour formed by 1st Battalion The Highland Light Infantry marches out of the Citadel in Cairo on 4 July 1946. The ceremony marked the formal handover of the Citadel to Egyptian control and was the first step towards ending British rule in Egypt.

depot became a giant recruiting hall and it took just sixteen hours to enlist the members of what would become the 15th (Tramways) Battalion, Highland Light Infantry.

Encouraged by that success, official approval was then given to the city's Boys' Brigade to form a 16th (Boys

Brigade) Battalion, a move that caused a great deal of public excitement in the city. 'Never will it be said that men who were connected with the Boys' Brigade throughout the length and breadth of the United Kingdom and Ireland funked in the hour of Britain's need,' noted a patriotic journalist in the *Glasgow Post*. A few days later, a third HLI 'pals' battalion, numbered 17th, was formed at the instigation of the Glasgow Chamber of Commerce with recruits being enrolled in the Lesser Hall of the Merchants House before parading, still in their city suits outside, the Stock Exchange.

That togetherness reaped a bitter harvest during the Battle of the Somme in the summer of 1916 when all three battalions were in action throughout the five-month battle and suffered heavy casualties. Among those who went over the top on the first day of the battle, 1 July, was the Treasurer of the Glasgow Boys' Brigade, Lieutenant Colonel David Laidlaw, command-ing 16th Highland Light Infantry, who remembered that his men were 'singing and whistling as if they were going to a football match instead of one of the most serious encounters in the world's history'. By the day's end 554 had been killed or wounded while carrying out their attack on a heavily defended German position known as the Leipzig Salient on the Thiepval Ridge. Scarcely an area of Glasgow was left unaffected and in the days that followed the casualty lists in the *Glasgow Herald* were thick with local names. The two other Volunteer battalions suffered equally grievously and, fittingly, the sacrifice of the 651 officers and men of the15th (Tramways) Battalion is commemorated by a memorial in the city's Transport Museum.

Paradoxically for such a quintessential Glasgow regiment, the HLI was formed in 1881 from two regiments which originally had little to do with the city or, indeed, the west of Scotland. The 71st (Highland) Foot was raised in 1777 by John Mackenzie, Lord Macleod, a member of a noted Jacobite family. Seventeen of its original officers were all called Mackenzie and at its first muster at Elgin in Moray its complement was predominantly Highland, from the ancestral lands of the Cromartie MacKenzies – Castle Leod, Coigach and Tarbat. All told, the new regiment consisted of 840 Highland Scots, 236 Lowland Scots and 38 Englishmen and Irishmen (some of these would have been Welsh). In 1809 the 71st was ordered to become a light infantry regiment and to adopt the rifle-green uniform, weapons and drill of similar regiments. When the regiment protested that it did not want to lose its Highland status the War Office relented and conceded that 'there is no objection to the 71st being denominated Highland Light Infantry Regiment, or to the retaining of their pipes, and the Highland garb for their pipers'. Initially the men wore regulation green light infantry trousers but in 1834 they started wearing trews in Lamont tartan.

In 1787 the second of the HLI's antecedent regiments, 74th Highlanders, came into being for service in India. Its first Colonel was Major General Sir Archibald Campbell of Inverneil in Argyllshire, who was serving at the time as Governor of Madras, and the management of recruitment, mainly from Lorne and Cowal, was left in the hands of his brothers and Lieutenant Colonel Gordon Forbes. Recruiting was a problem and the 74th was forced to take on more than 300 Lowland Scots but it was still counted as a Highland regiment and wore the government tartan. From the outset the new regiment decided to base its headquarters in Glasgow, in the old barracks in the Gallowgate, thereby beginning the long association between the city and the HLI. Shrewdly, as the commanding officer pointed out at the time, Glasgow was home to many Highlanders and men from the Western Isles who had gone there looking for work.

In 1803, while serving in India during the Mahratta campaign, the 74th took part in the Battle of Assaye under the command of the Hon. Arthur Wellesley (later the Duke of Wellington). Following victory, the three British regiments involved in the battle were given the unique honour of being allowed to carry a third Colour, the Assaye Colour, which is of white silk bearing the figure of an elephant surrounded by a laurel wreath and the name Assaye.

After the amalgamation of the two regiments in 1881, the HLI served in Egypt and India and in December 1899 the 1st Battalion was involved in the disastrous setback at Magersfontein during the Boer War when the highly regarded Highland Brigade was defeated by a smaller Boer force. While in the UK, the two battalions were frequently based at the regimental depot which was housed in Maryhill Barracks in Glasgow. Built on the Ruchill estate in the north of Glasgow and opened in 1872 to meet the need for a larger military presence in the city, the barracks occupied a fifty-four-acre site and throughout its time Maryhill had the feel of a garrison town. By the 1960s the barracks had become obsolete and were demolished to make way for the Wyndford housing estate. All that remains is the original gatehouse.

Maryhill Barracks' other claim to fame is that it was used to interrogate the Nazi deputy leader Rudolf Hess following his mysterious flight to Scotland in 1941.

During the Second World War the regiment supplied two Regular battalions and four Territorial battalions, one of which, the 9th, operated under the title Glasgow Highlanders. Curiously for a regiment with 'Highland' in its title, the HLI was not granted leave to wear the kilt until 1947. One of the regiment's most famous soldiers was Major General Roy Urquhart who commanded the 1st Airborne Division at Arnhem in September 1944 and who had joined 1st HLI in 1920. While the battalion was stationed in Malta he befriended a newly enlisted subaltern, the future actor and Hollywood star David Niven, whose presence had not been universally welcomed. Asked to list his preference of regiment while a cadet at Sandhurst, Niven had written as his third choice 'anything but the HLI' and was duly commissioned in them.

In 1959 The Highland Light Infantry amalgamated with The Royal Scots Fusiliers (21st) to form The Royal Highland Fusiliers and the new regiment retained its links with Glasgow through its headquarters in Sauchiehall Street. With the formation of The Royal Regiment of Scotland in 2006 it became the new regiment's 2nd Battalion.

# Battle Honours

## Pre-1914

*Carried on the Regimental Colour*
**Rolica, Vimiera, Corunna, Fuentes d'Onor, Almaraz, Vittoria, Pyrenees, Nive, Orthes, Peninsula, Waterloo, Sevastopol, Carnatic, Sholinghur, Mysore, Hindoostan, Central India, Cape of Good Hope, Tel-el-Kebir, Egypt, Modder River, South Africa, 1899–1902**

## First World War (26 battalions)

*Those in bold carried on the Queen's Colour*
**Mons,** Retreat from Mons, Marne 1914, Aisne 1914, **Ypres 1914, 15, 17, 18,** Langemarck 1914, 17, Gheluvelt, Nonnne Bosschen, Givency 1914, Neuve Chapelle, St Julien, Aubers, Festubert 1915, **Loos, Somme 1916, 18,** Albert 1916, 18, Bazentin, Delville Wood, Pozieres, Flers-Courcelette, Le Transloy, Ancre Heights, Ancre 1916, **Arras, 1917, 18,** Vimy 1917, Scarpe 1917, 18, Arleux, Pilckem, Menin Road, Polygon Wood, Passchendaele, Cambrai 1917, 18, St Quentin, Bapaume 1918, Lys, Estaires, Messines, 1918, Hazebrouck, Bailleul, Kemmel, Amiens, Drocourt-Queant, **Hindenburg Line,** Havrincourt, Canal du Nord, St Quentin Canal, Beaurevoir, Courtrai, Selle, Sambre, France and Flanders 1914–18, **Gallipoli 1915–18,** Rumani, Egypt 1916, Gaza, El Mughar, Nebi Samwil, Jaffa, **Palestine 1917–18,** Tigris 1916, Kut al Amara 1917, Sharqat, **Mesopotamia 1916–18,** Murman 1919, **Archangel 1919**

## Second World War

*Those in bold carried on the Queen's Colour*
Withdrawal to Cherbourg, **Odon,** Cheux, Esquay, Mont Pincon, Quarry Hill, Estry, Falaise, Seine 1944, Alart,

Nederrijn, Best, **Scheldt**, Lower Maas, South Beveland,
**Walcheren Causeway**, Asten, Roer, Ourthe, Rhineland,
**Reichswald**, Goch, Moyland Wood, Weeze, **Rhine**,
Ibbenburen, Dreierwalde, Aller, Uelzen, Bremen, Artlenberg,
**North-West Europe 1940, 44–45,** Jebel Shiba, Barentu,
**Keren**, Massawa, Abyssinia 1941, Gazala, **Cauldron**, Mersa
Matruh, Fuka, North Africa 1940–42, **Landing in Sicily**,
Sicily 1943, Italy 1943, 45, Athens, **Greece 1944–45**,
Adriatic, Middle East 1944.

The Battalion carried a third colour when on parade –
the Assaye Colour, the original of which was presented to the
74th Highlanders by the Honourable East India Company to
recognise the part they played in the Battle of Assaye in 1803.

## Recipients of the Victoria Cross

Private George Rodgers, 71st, Indian Mutiny, 1858
Lieutenant (later Major) William Mordaunt Marsh Edwards,
    2nd Battalion, Egypt, 1882
Captain the Hon. Alexander Gore Arkwright Hore-Ruthven
    (later the Earl of Gowrie), 3rd Battalion, Sudan, 1898
Corporal (later Bugle Major) John David Francis Shaul,
    1st Battalion, Boer War, 1899
Private Charles Kennedy, 1st Battalion, Boer War, 1900
Private George Wilson, 2nd Battalion, First World War, 1914
Lieutenant (later Lieutenant Colonel) Walter Lorrain Brodie,
    2nd Battalion, First World War, 1914
Lance Corporal William Angus, 8th Battalion, First World
    War, 1915
Sergeant James Youll Turnbull, 17th Battalion, First World
    War, 1916
Lance Corporal (later Colonel) John Brown Hamilton,
    9th Battalion, First World War, 1917

## The Highland Light Infantry

Lieutenant Colonel William Herbert Anderson,
  12th Battalion, First World War, 1918
Corporal (later Sergeant) David Ferguson Hunter,
  5th Battalion, First World War, 1918
Major Frank Gerald Blaker, The Highland Light Infantry,
  attached 3rd Battalion, 9th Gurkha Rifles, Second World
  War, 1944

# The Gordon Highlanders

## 75th and 92nd

Renowned as 'The Gay and Gallant Gordons', The Gordon Highlanders recruited from the city of Aberdeen and from the surrounding counties in the north-east of Scotland. Dotted throughout the regimental area are scores of granite-clad war memorials, many of them featuring the figure of a kilted Highland soldier, which testify not only to the north-east's sacrifices in two world wars but also to the community's close connections with the local regiment. The civic memorial in Keith is a good example, showing a defiant Gordon Highlander with a German *Pickelhaube* helmet trampled in the mud at his feet. The Gordons' motto said it all: 'Bydand', meaning 'enduring'.

The regiment's personality was formed from the fishing and farming communities that give the area its character – tough, unyielding, reticent of speech and blessed with an idiosyncratic sense of humour. More Victoria Crosses were won by Gordon Highlanders than by any other Scottish regiment; its battle honours were a roll call of campaigns fought by the British Army over two centuries and the distinctive yellow stripe in its government tartan kilt was widely known and respected. It also gave the army some of its finest soldiers, among whom may be mentioned Field Marshal George White, the winner of a Victoria Cross, and General Sir Ian Hamilton, the commander of the ill-fated Gallipoli campaign in 1915, who was twice turned down for the same award, on the first occasion because he was considered too young and the second because he was too senior. Another fine and upstanding Gordon Highlander was Major General Sir Hector Macdonald, who, unusually, rose from the ranks to become one of the best known soldiers of the late Victorian period. In more recent times the regiment was memorialised in the fictional Private McAuslan stories written by George MacDonald Fraser, who served in the 2nd Battalion immediately after the Second World War.

The regiment also gave rise to a popular music hall ditty in which 'Geordie Mackay of the HLI' is rejected while courting because he serves in the wrong regiment. The girl's catchy response in the chorus is the final put-down:

> A Gordon for me, a Gordon for me,
> If you're no' a Gordon, you're no use to me.
> The Black Watch are braw, the Seaforth an' a',
> But the cocky wee Gordons the pride of them a'.

Also inspired by the regiment was the catchphrase 'The Gordons will take it', which enjoyed a wide currency at the end of the nineteenth century. Before the storming of a well-defended enemy position at the Heights of Dargai in India's troublesome North-West Frontier Province in 1897, the commanding officer of 1st Gordons, Lieutenant Colonel H. H. Mathias, told his men: 'The General [Sir William Lockhart] says this hill must be taken at all costs

– the Gordon Highlanders will take it.' Before long, wags in London's gentlemen's clubs were saying that the same thing would happen if anyone left an umbrella unattended – 'the Gordons will take it'. As the Gordons stormed into the attack at Dargai, Piper George Findlater won a gallant Victoria Cross, continuing to play his bagpipes even though he had been wounded in both legs. His regiment succeeded in taking the position and the action was widely reported, turning the piper into a national hero. After leaving the army, Findlater settled down to farm at Forglen in Banffshire, where he died in 1942, aged seventy. He is buried in Forglen churchyard, near Turiff.

The history of the Gordons also embraces another fine regiment, the 75th (Stirlingshire) Foot, with which it amalgamated in 1881. Although the 75th had a distinguished record of service it more or less disappeared from history and very little is known about its foundation or its antecedents. At the time of the amalgamation the 75th had already lost its Highland status and, while it became the 1st Battalion of the new regiment, it is fair to say that when The Gordon Highlanders came into being in 1881 it was not so much an amalgamation of equals as a hostile takeover by a younger but better known regiment.

Given its subsequent history and achievements it is not really surprising that the story of the raising of the 92nd (Highland) Regiment is steeped in romance. Its founder was Alexander, 4th Duke of Gordon, a north-east landowner, who raised a regiment in 1794 for service in the war against France. Originally designated the 100th Foot, it was quickly associated with the Gordon family but from the outset recruiting proved troublesome, so much so that the Duke had to introduce a cash bounty to encourage his tenants to join up. Regimental records provide a graphic account of the way in which every recruit had his price. Two young men from the Badenoch district received £21 and one recruit in Peterhead was given £24. Almost £2,500 was paid out in bounties from the Duke's exchequer at Gordon Castle in Banffshire – an enormous sum worth around £225,000 today.

The payment of the additional bounty created a romantic myth around the raising of the regiment and the part by played by the Duke's wife, Jean, Duchess of Gordon, a lady of undoubted charm and beauty who introduced a novel way of recruiting. Throughout the summer of 1794 she rode around the surrounding countryside visiting local fairs where she offered a kiss and a golden guinea to any man who agreed to join up. Many accepted the offer, including a young blacksmith in Huntly remarkable for his strength and good looks. Recruiters from other regiments including the Foot Guards had attempted without success to enlist him, but he could not resist the Duchess. He took the kiss and the guinea; but to show that it was not the gold that had tempted him he tossed the coin into the crowd. While the story's authenticity has been disputed, it still forms a key part of the regiment's history simply because it is such a good tale.

The new regiment was soon in action in continental Europe and played a notable role at Waterloo in 1815. The moment came during an attack by the heavy cavalry of the Union Brigade when the Royal Scots Greys piled into the advancing French with the pipes of the Gordons

Men of the Gordon Highlanders suffer the indignity of being taken prisoner by the Germans during the First World War. They probably served in the 1st Battalion which had the misfortune to surrender after being outnumbered in confused fighting during the retreat from Mons in August 1914.

playing and shouts of 'Scotland For Ever' ringing in their ears. For the Greys the attack meant that they had to advance through the lines of their fellow countrymen and it is possible that Gordon Highlanders joined in the charge by clinging to the stirrups of the cavalry as they swept past them. Later an officer confided that his 'Highlanders seemed half mad, and it was with the greatest difficulty the officers could preserve anything like order in the ranks'.

That willingness to engage in battle whatever the odds was typical of the Gordon Highlanders throughout its 200-year existence. During the Boer War the future Prime Minister Winston Churchill called it 'the finest regiment in the world' after watching 1st Gordons going into the attack at Doornkop, and during the First World War it raised twenty battalions for service on all the main battlefronts. Above all, the regiment remained very much a product of the indomitable spirit evinced by the men of the north-east of Scotland who served in its ranks. During the fighting in Sicily in 1943 a platoon from 5th/7th Gordons was surrounded by the Germans and ordered to surrender. It was to no avail; a rich Aberdonian voice responded: 'Come and get us ye feart [scared] fucker!'

By the 1970s oil had been discovered in the North Sea, sparking a jobs bonanza in the north-east of Scotland. As a result fewer young men saw opportunities in a military career and recruitment into the Gordons slumped. Largely as a result of that downturn, in 1994, its bicentenary, the Gordons amalgamated with Queen's Own Highlanders to form The Highlanders (Seaforth, Gordon and Cameron) and in 2006 it became the 4th Battalion The Royal Regiment of Scotland.

# Battle Honours

## Pre-1914

*Carried on the Regimental Colour*

**Mysore, Seringapatam, Egmont-op-Zee, Mandora, Corunna Fuentes d'Onor, Almarez, Vittoria, Nive, Orthes, Pyrenees, Peninsula, Waterloo, South Africa 1835, Chitral, Delhi 1857, Lucknow, Charasiah, Kabul 1879, Kandahar 1880, Afghanistan 1878–80, Tel-el-Kebir, Egypt 1882, 84, Nile 1884–85, Tirah, Defence of Ladysmith, Paardeberg, South Africa 1899–1902**

## First World War (21 battalions)

*Those in bold carried on the Queen's Colour*

**Mons, Le Cateau,** Retreat from Mons, **Marne 1914, 18,** Aisne, 1914, La Bassee 1914, Messines 1914, Armentieres 1914, **Ypres 1914, 15, 17,** Langemarck 1914, Gheluvelt, Nonne Boschen, Neuve Chapelle, Frezenberg, Bellewaarde, Aubers, Festubert 1915, Hooge 1915, **Loos, Somme 1916, 18,** Albert 1916, 18, Bazentin, Delville Wood, Pozieres, Guillemont, Flers-Courcelette, Le Transloy, **Ancre 1916, Arras 1917, 18,** Vimy 1917, Scarpe 1917, 18, Arleux, Bullecourt, Pilckem, Menin Road, Polygon Wood, Broodseinde, Poelcapelle, Passchendaele, **Cambrai 1917, 18,** St Quentin, Bapaume 1918, Rosieres, Lys, Estaires, Hazebrouck, Bethune, Soissonais-Ourcq, Tardenois, Hindenburg Line, Canal du Nord, Selle, Sambres, France and Flanders 1914–18, Piave, **Vittorio Veneto,** Italy 1917–18

## Second World War

*Those in bold carried on the Queen's Colour*

Withdrawal to Escaut, Ypres-Comines Canal, Dunkirk 1940, Somme 1940, St Valery-en-Caux, **Odon,** La Vie Crossing,

Lower Maas, Venlo Pocket, Rhineland, **Reichswald,**
Cleve, **Goch, Rhine, North-West Europe 1940, 44–45,**
**El Alamein,** Advance on Tripoli, **Mareth,** Medjez Plain,
**North Africa 1942–43,** Landing in Sicily, **Sferro,** Sicily 1943,
**Anzio,** Rome, Italy 1944–45

## Recipients of the Victoria Cross

Private Thomas Beach, 92nd Highlanders, Crimean War, 1854

Ensign (later Colonel) Richard Wadeson, 75th Foot,
  Indian Mutiny, 1857

Private (later Colour Sergeant) Patrick Green,
  75th Foot, Indian Mutiny, 1857

Colour Sergeant Cornelius Coghlan (also Coughlan),
  75th Foot, Indian Mutiny, 1857

Major (later Field Marshal) George White, 92nd Highlanders,
  Afghanistan, 1879

Lieutenant (later Lieutenant Colonel) William Henry Dick-
  Cunyngham, 92nd Highlanders, Afghanistan, 1879

Private Edward Lawson, 1st Battalion, India, 1897

Piper George Findlater, 1st Battalion, India, 1897

Captain (later Major) Matthew Meiklejohn, 2nd Battalion,
  Boer War, 1899

Sergeant Major (later Lieutenant Colonel) William Robertson,
  2nd Battalion, Boer War, 1899

Captain Ernest Towse, 1st Battalion, Boer War, 1900

Lance Corporal (later Lieutenant Colonel) John Frederick
  Mackay, 1st Battalion, Boer War, 1900

Captain (later Colonel) William Eagleston Gordon,
  1st Battalion, Boer War, 1900

Captain David Reginald Younger, 1st Battalion, Boer War, 1900

Drummer (later Drum Major) William Kenny, 2nd Battalion,
  First World War, 1914

Lieutenant James Anson Ortho Brooke, 2nd Battalion, First World War, 1914

Private George Imlach McIntosh, 1/6th Battalion, First World War, 1917

Lieutenant (later Major) Allan Ebenezer Kerr, 3rd Battalion, First World War, 1918

Moving up to the front line: 2nd Battalion The Gordon Highlanders march along the road to Fricourt during the later stages of the Battle of the Somme in October 1916.

# The Royal Dublin Fusiliers

## 102nd and 103rd

Together with three other southern Irish regiments – The Connaught Rangers, The Prince of Wales's Leinster Regiment (Royal Canadians) and The Royal Munster Fusiliers – The Royal Dublin Fusiliers had a relatively short existence within the British Army, all having been formed in 1881 and disbanded in 1922 at the time of the creation of the Irish Free State. (The other Irish regiment to be disbanded at the same time was The Royal Irish Regiment, which had been formed in 1684.) Within those forty-one years, though, The Royal Dublin Fusiliers received the battle honours 'South Africa 1899–1902' and 'Siege of Ladysmith' for service in the Boer War, as well as forty-eight battle honours during the First World War when three of its men were awarded the Victoria Cross. Their sacrifice and that of 49,400 Irish soldiers in the First World War is commemorated in the Irish National War Memorial Gardens in Dublin, some three miles from the city centre close to Phoenix Park and Kilmainham Hill. Designed by Sir Edwin Lutyens, it comprises a sunken Garden of Remembrance whose centrepiece is a huge granite Stone of Remembrance and two pairs of pergolas also in granite, representing the four provinces of Ireland, and containing illuminated volumes recording the names of all the dead. The restored Gardens were rededicated on 10 September 1988.

Although the regiment's history was only short-lived within the British Army, its antecedents went back to the seventeenth century when the Honourable East India Company formed the Madras European Regiment in 1648 and the Bombay Regiment 1661. Two centuries later these became the 102nd Royal Madras Fusiliers and the 103rd Royal Bombay Fusiliers before they were amalgamated in 1881 as The Royal Dublin Fusiliers, having been brought into the British military establishment following the mutiny of 1857. Because of the length of time they had served in India, The Royal Dublin Fusiliers were known as 'The Old Toughs', but they also answered to their local nickname 'The Dubs'. As a fusilier regiment the men wore a uniform that included a cap made of black bear or racoon skin with a blue and green plume on the left side while the front of the cap carried the regimental badge of a grenade surmounted with a tiger above an elephant. The base for the regiment was a newly built depot and barracks at Naas in County Kildare, Ireland, and its official recruiting counties were designated as Dublin, Kildare, Wicklow and Carlow. After independence in 1922 and the disbandment of the regiment, the buildings remained in public use and served as the Army Apprentice School in the 1950s, but Devoy Barracks (as it had become) closed in 1998 when new county buildings were constructed on the site.

Little remains of the physical presence of the British Army in Naas and in the aftermath of Ireland's independence it was considered almost shameful to acknowledge the role played by British regiments such as

Men of a battalion of The Royal Dublin Fusiliers march through the rain somewhere in Ireland, probably before embarking for service in France during the First World War.

The Royal Dublin Fusiliers. However, all was not entirely lost: as if to demonstrate that regiments never really die but continue to live on in people's hearts, a Royal Dublin Fusiliers Association (RDFA) was formed in Dublin in January 1997 following an exhibition mounted in the Dublin Civic Museum in South William Street to acknowledge the role played by the regiment during the First World War. With eighty founding members, by 2012 that membership had grown to 1,251, the chairman noting at the time that 'much like the old regiment itself, the bulk of the membership of the RDFA came from a cross-section of Irish society'.

It was fitting that the wartime service of so many Irishmen should have been commemorated for, in common with all British infantry regiments, The Royal Dublin Fusiliers expanded substantially to meet the challenge of raising recruits for service during the First World War. As Irish infantry regiments did not include Territorial battalions in their Orders of Battle, The Royal Dublin Fusiliers relied on raising volunteers from all over Ireland, creating seven Service battalions for service in Gallipoli and on the Western Front and three Garrison battalions of older soldiers, which served in India and on the Salonika front. Among the volunteers were 350 Dublin rugby union players who paraded at the Lansdowne Road ground and then marched to the huge military camp at The Curragh where they formed D Company of 7th Royal Dublin Fusiliers. They were promptly christened 'The Toffs in the Old Toughs'. Among them was Ernest Julian, a barrister and Reid Professor of Law at Trinity College, Dublin, who was killed in action at Gallipoli in August 1915. Another rifle company in the same battalion was composed of 'Larkinites', Dublin dockers who had supported their radical union leader, James Larkin, in the famous 'lock-out' and strike of the previous year.

Perhaps the most remarkable of the many volunteers was Father William Doyle, a Jesuit padre who served with 8th Royal Dublin Fusiliers on the Western Front. Born in the suburb of Dalkey, the youngest of seven children, Doyle entered the Jesuit Novitiate at the age of eighteen and on the outbreak of war immediately joined the army as a padre. While serving on the Western Front he gained a well-deserved reputation both for his bravery under fire and for his refusal to make any distinction between soldiers of different faiths. One Ulster Protestant officer later said that Father Doyle 'didn't know the meaning of fear and he didn't know what bigotry was'. In 1916 he was awarded a Military Cross – an unusual distinction for a padre – but he was killed during the Third Battle of Ypres on 16 August 1917, having run 'all day hither and thither over the battlefield like an angel of mercy'. During the conflict the Dubs lost 4,700 men killed and thousands more were wounded.

Perhaps the most painful incident involving the regiment came during the Easter Rising in 1916. When the nationalist rebellion began in Dublin on 24 April, 10th Royal Dublin Fusiliers was in residence at the Royal Barracks, later to become Collins Barracks (named after Michael Collins, the first commander-in-chief of the Irish Free State) and now part of the National Museum of Ireland. At the time the battalion was preparing to deploy to the Western Front and was immediately involved in the operations to relieve Dublin Castle. The following day the 5th Battalion arrived

The tug-of-war team of The Royal Dublin Fusiliers in 1914.
The British Army favoured the tug-of-war as an ideal way of
building up physical strength while simultaneously fostering
co-operation and teamwork.

in the city from the Curragh, travelling by train, and they engaged the rebels at the City Hall. Also in action in that period was the 4th Battalion, which travelled to the city from Richmond Barracks at Templemore in County Tipperary and took part in the fighting along the railway line from the Broadstone railway station held by the rebels, up to the Cabra Bridge. Once an important transport hub serving the west of Ireland, the station closed in 1961 and only its façade remains.

All told, the regiment lost two officers and ten other ranks during the fighting in Dublin but despite the provocation and the risk of conflicting loyalties, the three battalions remained loyal. Later John Dillon MP, leader of the Irish Parliamentary Party, informed the House of Commons that he had asked Ireland's commander-in-chief, Lieutenant General Sir John Maxwell, 'Have you any cause of complaint of the Dublins [The Royal Dublin Fusiliers] who had to go down and fight their own people in the streets of Dublin? Did a single man turn back and betray the uniform he wears?' To which Maxwell replied, 'Not a man.'

---

## Battle Honours

### Pre-1914

*Carried on the Regimental Colour*
Arcot, Plassey, Condore, Wandiwash, Pondicherry, Buxar, Guzerat, Carnatic, Mysore, Seringapatam, Nundy Droog, Amboyna, Ternate, Banda, Maheidpoor,Kirkee, Beni Boo Ali, Aden, Mooltan, Goojerat, Punjaub, Ava, Pegu, Lucknow, Siege of Ladysmith, South Africa 1899–1902

## First World War (11 battalions)

*Those in bold are carried on the Queen's Colour*
Le Cateau, **Retreat from Mons, Marne 1914,** Aisne 1914,
Armentiéres 1914, **Ypres 1915, 17, 18,** St Julien, Frezenberg,
Bellewaarde, **Somme 1916, 18,** Albert 1916, Guillemont,
Ginchy, Le Transloy, Ancre 1916, Arras 1917, Scarpe 1917,
Arleux, Messines 1917, Langemarck 1917, Polygon Wood,
**Cambrai 1917, 18,** St Quentin, Bapaume 1918, Rosières, Avre,
**Hindenburg Line,** St Quentin Canal, Beaurevoir, Courtrai,
**Selle,** Sambre, France and Flanders 1914–18, Kosturino,
Struma, **Macedonia 1915–17,** Helles, Landing at Helles,
Krithia, Suvla, Sari Bair, Landing at Suvla, Scimitar Hill,
**Gallipoli 1915–16,** Egypt 1916, Gaza, Jerusalem, Tell 'Asur,
**Palestine 1917–18**

## Recipients of the Victoria Cross

Sergeant Robert Downie, 2nd Battalion, First World War, 1916
Sergeant James Ockendon, 1st Battalion, First World War, 1916
Private (later Sergeant) Sergeant Horace Augustus Curtis,
    2nd Battalion, First World War, 1918

# The Rifle Brigade (Prince Consort's Own)

Contrary to what may be implied by its title – a brigade is normally a grouping of infantry battalions – The Rifle Brigade was a regiment with a conceit worthy of its abilities. Its spirit was captured by Bernard Cornwell in his best-selling Sharpe novels and the regiment enjoyed many unique distinctions during its 158 years of existence. Formed in 1800 as an 'Experimental Corps of Riflemen', or the 95th Rifle Regiment, to provide the army with elite troops who would act as sharpshooters, scouts and skirmishers, it enjoyed a close association with the Duke of Wellington on whose orders it was taken out of the numbered Regiments of the Line in 1816 and named The Rifle Brigade with four operational battalions.

Although the regiment disappeared in 1958, when it began the first of several amalgamations, many of its traditions live on in The Rifles, which was formed in 2007 from the army's rifle and light infantry regiments. The Rifle Brigade is represented in the 4th Battalion and there are other long-standing connections with the past. The Rifles still has its headquarters at Peninsula Barracks in Winchester, which is also home to several military museums as well as an exclusive private housing development. Winchester was also the headquarters of another notable rifle regiment, The King's Royal Rifle

Corps (60th), which is another constituent part of The Rifles.

Some idea of the sense of elitism and disciplined informality central to the ethos of The Rifle Brigade can be found in the fictional figure of the maverick Richard Sharpe who serves in the 95th during its campaigns in the Peninsula during the Napoleonic Wars. In an early episode Sharpe greets the men assigned to him and makes it clear that they will have to prove themselves to his satisfaction before he accepts them. The accuracy of Cornwell's depiction is confirmed by *Recollections of Rifleman Harris*, a memoir written by Benjamin Randell Harris, a young man from Hampshire who joined the newly formed 95th in Ireland. Although illiterate, his recollections were recorded and transcribed by Captain Henry Curling in the 1830s and they remain one of the best introductions to life as a private soldier in Wellington's army. Harris is particularly astute about the regiment's role in the Peninsular War where the concept of the light infantry came into its own. He said of that time: 'I enjoyed life more whilst on active service than I have ever done since, and I look back on my time spent on the fields of the Peninsula as the only part worthy of remembrance.'

With their smart green uniforms and the rapid marching style of 140 paces per minute, The Rifle Brigade cut fine figures on parade and in common with other rifle regiments they carried no colours. To transmit commands in battle, the battalions in The Rifle Brigade used bugles instead of the drums employed by line infantry for the same purpose. There was also a marked difference in tactics: riflemen were trained to work in open order ahead of the main infantry formations and were encouraged to

Surviving members of the original 2nd Battalion The Rifle Brigade which crossed over to France in 1914 with the British Expeditionary Force. They left behind them 800 casualties buried in France and Flanders.

think for themselves. They were taught to make best use of natural cover and to harass the enemy with aimed shots instead of relying on the mass volley and the use of bayonet for close-quarter killing. Their weapons were also different: whereas the infantry of the line used the reliable Brown Bess musket, men of The Rifle Brigade were issued with the modern Baker rifle which had a longer range and was considerably more accurate. During the Peninsular War, Rifleman Thomas Plunkett of the 1st Battalion shot the French general Auguste-Marie-François Colbert de Chabanais at a range of over a hundred yards, a remarkable achievement at the time; Plunkett then shot a second French officer who rode to the general's aid, thus proving that the first shot was not a fluke. In 1852 the regiment was granted the title 'The Prince Consort's Own Rifle Brigade' in honour of HRH Prince Albert, husband of Queen Victoria.

To meet the need for men during the First World War, The Rifle Brigade raised twenty-eight battalions for service on the Western Front as well as in Salonika, where the 22nd Rifle Brigade had in its ranks more than sixty men over the age of sixty. The first two of twelve Victoria Crosses awarded to the regiment during the conflict were won by Company Sergeant Major Harry Daniels and Acting Corporal Cecil Reginald Noble, both 2nd Rifle Brigade, who advanced ahead of the battalion under heavy fire during the Battle of Neuve Chapelle on 12 March 1915 and successfully cut the barbed wire blocking the advance. Four months later, on 30 July 1915, a third VC was awarded to 2nd Lieutenant Sidney Clayton Woodroffe, 8th Rifle Brigade, for his courageous defence of a position at Hooge on the Ypres sector. His death was commemorated by the poet Charles Hamilton Sorley who had been at Marlborough College with him:

There is no fitter end than this.
No need is now to yearn nor sigh.
We know the glory that is his,
A glory that can never die.

Woodroffe's older brother Kenneth served in 6th Rifle Brigade and was a first-class cricketer who played for Sussex and Cambridge University. He was killed in action on 9 May 1915. The regiment was also home to one of only three father and son recipients of the VC in the British Army: Major Billy Congreve for his leadership at Longueval on the Somme and his father, General Walter Congreve, who received his award at Colenso in December 1899 during the Boer War. To reflect the large numbers of Londoners who joined The Rifle Brigade during the war, the regiment's memorial to the '11,576 Officers, Non-Commissioned Officers and Riflemen of the Rifle Brigade Who Fell in the Great War 1914–1918' stands in Grosvenor Gardens, Victoria, London. Designed by John Tweed, it was unveiled in 1920 and contains three figures representing a rifleman of the conflict and an officer and rifleman of the early nineteenth century.

At the outbreak of the Second World War the regiment's tradition of speed and initiative in battle was instrumental in the decision to give its regular battalions a motorised role during the early fighting in France. That could not save the 1st Battalion, however, which was forced to surrender at Calais on 26 May 1940 after putting up a stubborn defence against superior numbers, but it was

Men of a battalion of The Rifle Brigade being trained on a Bren gun, in the period between the two world wars.

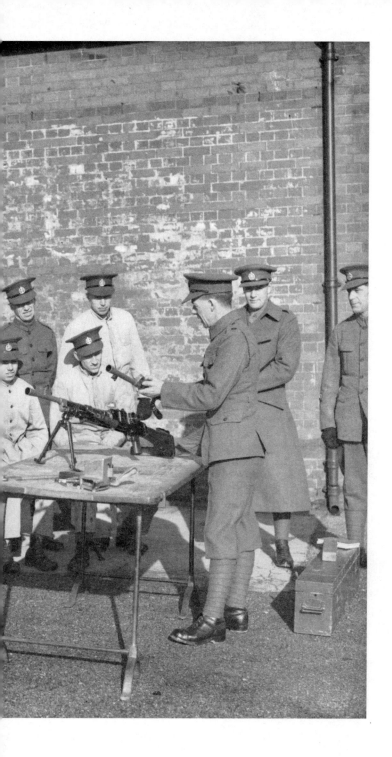

re-formed and went on to serve with great gallantry alongside the 2nd Battalion in North Africa. Four other battalions served in the Italian campaign and at the end of the conflict the regiment was awarded fifty-seven battle honours.

Given The Rifle Brigade's reputation as an elite regiment it is not surprising that it has produced a fair number of outstanding officers, including General Sir Henry Wilson, Chief of the Imperial General Staff in 1918, and General Sir Frank Kitson, an expert on modern low-intensity warfare. Among the more flamboyant soldiers who served in The Rifle Brigade was Neil 'Bunny' Roger, a well-known couturier and dandy whose dress-making business in London attracted an international clientele, including many of the most famous film stars of the day. During the fighting in Italy in 1944 he claimed to have gone into action wearing a chiffon scarf and carrying a copy of the fashion magazine *Vogue*; on another occasion he allegedly responded to a sergeant's question regarding approaching German infantrymen with his stock phrase, 'When in doubt, powder heavily.'

---

## Battle Honours

Rifle regiments did not carry Colours

### Pre-1914

Copenhagen, Monte Video, Rolica, Vimiera, Corunna, Busaco, Barrosa, Fuentes d'Onor, Ciudad Rodrigo, Badajoz, Salamanca, Vittoria, Pyrenees, Nivelle, Nive, Orthes, Toulouse,

# The Rifle Brigade (Prince Consort's Own)

Peninsula, Waterloo, South Africa 1846–47, South Africa 1851–2–3, Alma, Inkerman, Sevastopol, Lucknow, Ashantee 1873–74, Ali Masjid, Afghanistan 1878–79, Burma 1885–87, Khartoum, Defence of Ladysmith, Relief of Ladysmith, South Africa 1899–1902

## First World War (28 battalions)

Le Cateau, Retreat from Mons, Marne 1914, Aisne 1914, 18, Armentières 1914, Neuve Chapelle, Ypres 1915, 17, Gravenstafel, St. Julien, Frezenberg, Bellewaarde, Aubers, Hooge 1915, Somme 1916, 18, Albert 1916, 18, Bazentin, Delville Wood, Guillemont, Flers-Courcelette, Morval, Le Transloy, Ancre Heights, Ancre 1916, 18, Arras 1917, 18, Vimy 1917, Scarpe 1917, 18, Arleux, Messines 1917, Pilckem, Langemarck 1917, Menin Road, Polygon Wood, Broodseinde, Poelcappelle, Passchendaele, Cambrai 1917, 18, St. Quentin, Rosières, Avre, Villers Bretonneux, Lys, Hazebrouck, Béthune, Drocourt-Quéant, Hindenburg Line, Havrincourt, Canal du Nord, Selle, Valenciennes, Sambre, France and Flanders 1914–18, Macedonia 1915–18

## Second World War

Calais 1940, Villers Bocage, Odon, Bourguébus Ridge, Mont Pincon, Le Perier Ridge, Falaise, Antwerp, Hechtel, Nederrijn, Lower Maas, Roer, Leese, Aller, North-West Europe 1940, 44–45, Egyptian Frontier 1940, Beda Fomm, Mersa el Brega, Agedabia, Derna Aerodrome, Tobruk 1941, Sidi Rezegh 1941, Chor es Sufan, Saunnu, Gazala, Knightsbridge, Defence of Alamein Line, Ruweisat, Alam el Halfa, El Alamein, Tebaga Gap, Medjez el Bab, Kassarine, Thala, Fondouk Pass, El Kourzia, Djebel Kournine, Tunis, Hammam Lif, North Africa 1940–43, Cardito, Cassino II, Liri Valley, Melfa Crossing, Monte Rotondo, Capture of Perugia, Monte Malbe,

Arezzo, Advance to Florence, Gothic Line, Orsara,
Tossigniano, Argenta Gap, Fossa Sembalina, **Italy 1943–45**

## Recipients of the Victoria Cross

Rifleman Francis Wheatley, 1st Battalion, Crimean War, 1854

Lieutenant (later Major General Sir) the Hon. Henry Hugh
   Clifford, The Rifle Brigade, Crimean War, 1854

Lieutenant (later Colonel Sir) William James Montgomery
   Cunninghame, 1st Battalion, Crimean War, 1854

Lieutenant (later Colonel) Claude Thomas Bourchier,
   1st Battalion, Crimean War, 1854

Rifleman (later Corporal) Joseph Bradshaw, 2nd Battalion,
   Crimean War, 1855

Rifleman Robert Humpston, 2nd Battalion, Crimean War, 1855

Rifleman (later Corporal) Roderick McGregor, 2nd Battalion,
   Crimean War, 1855

Lieutenant (later Brevet Major) John Simpson Knox,
   2nd Battalion, Crimean War, 1857

Captain (later Colonel) Henry Wilmot, 2nd Battalion,
   Indian Mutiny, 1858

Corporal (later Sergeant) William Nash, 2nd Battalion,
   Indian Mutiny, 1858

Rifleman David Hawkes, 2nd Battalion, Indian Mutiny, 1858

Rifleman (later Corporal) James Shaw, 3rd Battalion,
   Indian Mutiny, 1858

Rifleman, Timothy O'Hea, 1st Battalion, Canada, 1866

Captain (later General Sir) Walter Norris Congreve,
   The Rifle Brigade, Boer War, 1899

Rifleman (later Lance Corporal) Alfred Edward Durrant,
   2nd Battalion, Boer War, 1900

Brevet Major (later Brigadier) John Edmund Gough,
   The Rifle Brigade, Somaliland, 1903

Company Sergeant Major (later Lieutenant Colonel) Harry Daniels, 2nd Battalion, First World War, 1915

Acting Corporal Cecil Reginald Noble, 2nd Battalion, First World War, 1915

Lance Sergeant (later Captain) Douglas Walter Belcher, 1/5th Battalion, First World War, 1915

2nd Lieutenant Sidney Clayton Woodroffe, 8th Battalion, First World War, 1915

Corporal Alfred George Drake, 8th Battalion, First World War, 1915

Brevet Major William La Touche Congreve, The Rifle Brigade, First World War, 1916

2nd Lieutenant George Edward Cates, 2nd Battalion, First World War, 1917

Sergeant, William Francis Burman, 16th Battalion, First World War, 1917

Sergeant Arthur George Knight, 2nd/8th Battalion, First World War, 1917

Lance Sergeant (later Captain) Joseph Edward Woodall, 1st Battalion, First World War, 1918

Sergeant (later Company Sergeant Major) William Gregg, 13th Battlion, First World War, 1918

Rifleman (later Sergeant) William Beesley, 13th Battalion, First World War, 1918

Lieutenant Colonel Victor Buller Turner, 2nd Battalion, Second World War, 1942

# Picture Credits

Alamy – 12–13, 172–3, 176–7, 224–5, 239, 254–5,
  296–7, 302–3
Corbis – 42–3, 160–1, 208–9
Courtesy of the Fusilier Museum, Lancashire – 114–5,
  118, 119
Getty Images – 34–5, 46–7, 52–3, 57, 68–9, 74–5, 78;
  84–5, 88–9, 94–5, 99, 106–7, 144, 154–5, 164–5,
  182–3, 186–7, 196–7, 204–5, 216–7, 228–9
Imperial War Museum – 21, 140, 150–1, 248–9, 284,
  306–7, 320–1
Mary Evans Picture Library – 193, 214, 258–9, 266,
  274–5, 279, 316–7
National Army Museum – 24, 30–1, 64–5, 103, 234–5,
  244, 310–11
Royal Scots Museum – 14
The Regimental Museum of The Royal Welsh, Brecon –
  124–5, 127, 128–9, 131, 132–3

# Bibliography

All the regiments in this book have extensive historiographies which include well-researched regimental histories. The following provide readable accounts of the development of the regimental system within the British Army.

Ascoli, David, *A Companion to the British Army 1660–1983*, London, 1983

Barnett, Correlli, *Britain and her Army 1509–1970*, London, 1970

Brereton, J. M., *The British Army: A Social History of the British Army from 1661 to the Present Day*, London, 1986

Carver, Michael, *Seven Ages of the British Army*, London, 1986

Chandler, David, and Beckett, Ian, eds., *The Oxford Illustrated History of the British Army*, Oxford, 1994

David, Saul, *All the King's Men: The British Soldier from the Restoration to Waterloo*, London, 2013

Fortescue, Sir John, *A History of the British Army*, 13 vols, Macmillan, London, 1899–1930

Mallinson, Allan, *The Making of the British Army: From the English Civil War to the War on Terror*, London, 2009

Messenger, Charles, *For Love of Regiment: A History of British Infantry*, 2 vols, Barnsley, 1993–1994

Swinson, Arthur, ed., *A Register of the Regiments and Corps of the British Army: The Ancestry of the Regiments and Corps of the Regular Establishment of the Army*, London, 1972

# Index

Figures in *italic* indicate pictures.

# Index

# Index

# Index

# Index

# Index